Russian Origami

Russian Origami

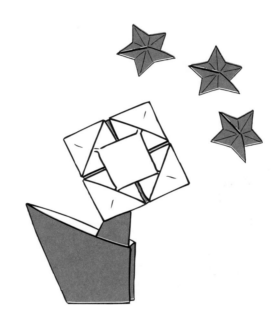

Sergei Afonkin
and Thomas Hull

St. Martin's Griffin

New York

Library of Congress Cataloging-in-Publication Data

Afonkin, Sergei.
   Russian origami / Sergei Afonkin and Thomas Hull.—1st ed.
     p. cm.
   ISBN 0-312-16993-0
   1. Origami — Russia (Federation) I. Hull, Thomas. II Title.
TT870.A34 1998
736'.982'0947—dc21

97-41444
CIP

First St. Martin's Griffin Edition: April 1998

10 9 8 7 6 5 4 3 2 1

To the Memory of Michael Shall

Fate never gave me the chance to meet this man, but the passion he gave to origami flew across the ocean, inspiring me to spread the art of paperfolding as far as I can, in a country on the opposite side of the globe.

—SERGEI AFONKIN, Russia

Michael's desire to share origami with every country and every person on the planet was a direct inspiration for this book. In these pages his spirit and his mission live on.

—THOMAS HULL, USA

Contents

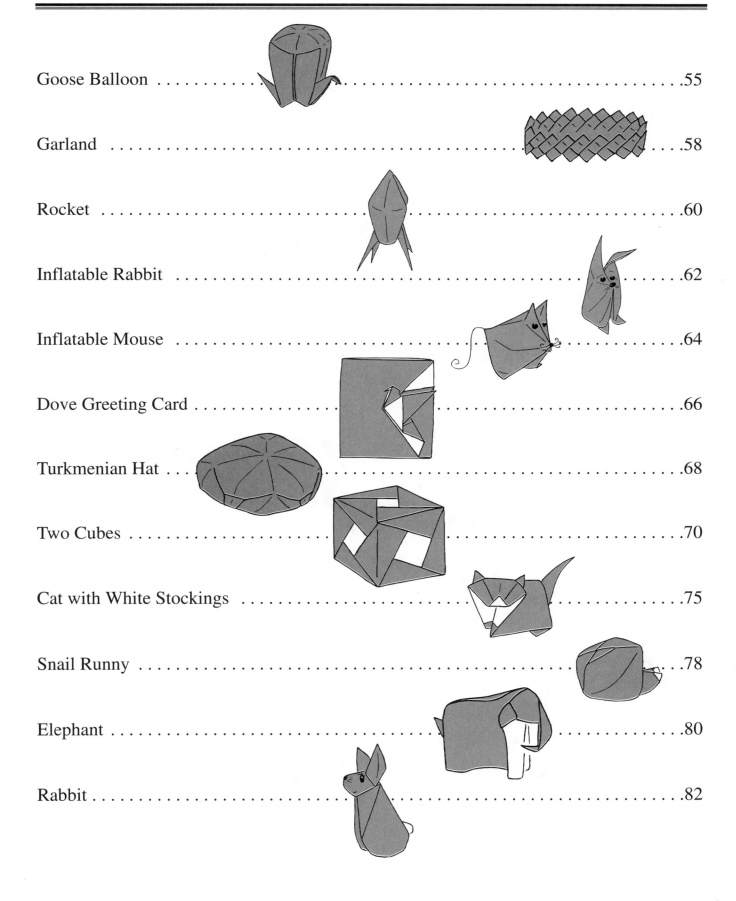

Preface

The story behind the creation of this book is quite remarkable. However, in order to appreciate it fully one needs to know a few things about the origami community in the world today. Indeed, without the bigger picture one might easily wonder why a book titled *Russian Origami* would come into being in the first place!

Paperfolding has its roots in Japanese culture. The word "origami," after all, is Japanese, literally meaning "folded paper." As far back as the 1600s the Japanese were utilizing origami in their customs and traditions, but it wasn't until the twentieth century that paperfolding became a recreational pastime for people all over the world. This was largely due to the pioneering efforts of Akira Yoshizawa in Japan, Robert Harbin in England, and Lillian Oppenheimer in America, all of whom devoted much of their lives (or continue to do so, in the case of Master Yoshizawa!) to sharing the joys of paperfolding with the rest of the world. They, and numerous others, did this by teaching origami, developing new models, publishing origami books, arranging origami exhibitions and hosting origami conventions.

Much of this spreading of origami was facilitated by the creation of origami organizations. The foundation of The Friends of the Origami Center (now known as OrigamiUSA) in America and the British Origami Society in England was a crucial step, providing focal points for paperfolders in the West where information could be exchanged and origami books and paper could be obtained. Such efforts have spread to the Internet, and origami home pages now dot the webscape. The origami world is a busy place! I, myself, have contributed by becoming active in OrigamiUSA and by publishing a book with the American origami master Robert Neale, *Origami, Plain and Simple*.

Enthusiasts are always excited to see origami being practiced in other countries and in different cultures. Thus I was thrilled when I received an E-mail message in early 1996 from Sergei Afonkin, the Chairman of the St. Petersburg Origami Center. He was writing because his organization had a copy of my book and wanted information on our American origami conventions. I hadn't heard much about this new origami organization in the former Soviet Union, and was eager to use this introduction as an opportunity to learn more.

Sergei and I discovered that we had much in common, besides origami. We are both avid teachers, he of biology and I of mathematics. We are both interested in the geometry of origami, and both of us plan to write books on the subject. It is quite a feeling to discover that you have a "soul-relation"—an alter ego of sorts—on the other side of the world, one whom you never would have discovered were it not for the marvel of writing books, letters, and E-mail.

As our E-mail friendship grew I learned that Sergei is an insatiable advocate of origami—one of these people who make things happen by their sheer enthusiasm. He would E-mail me about conventions he was planning, books he was developing with Russian publishers, and about his "origami database" of Russian-invented models. Since the conception of the St. Petersburg Origami Center (shortly after the breakup of the Soviet Union) Sergei has been collecting origami models that his Russian members have created. When he first told me of this, his database contained 600 models. Now he tells me that the number is up to 1000!

All this prepared me somewhat for Sergei's proposal that I help him write a book to be published in the West, containing Russian created origami models. "What a wonderful idea!" I thought. I tentatively agreed to the project, but I needed to actually see some of these models before I could commit myself. Sergei mailed (via the normal post) diagrams for over 50 models, all by Russian creators. I was astounded! The quality of the creations was incredible. Here was a wealth of models, all from the standard origami bases that we are all familiar with in the West. But these were new! Fold after fold I found amazingly creative uses of the basic origami forms that I knew and loved. "Why had none of us thought of this before?!" was my recurring question as I explored these new folds. In short, I was hooked.

One may think that writing a book with someone halfway around the globe would be an inconvenience, if not impossible. It is safe to say that the book you hold in your hands was conceived, born, and raised on the Internet. Sergei and I began daily E-mail discussions to plan our book, with Sergei replying to my messages while I was deep asleep and vice versa. After we decided which models would be in the book and I

had secured the interest of our publisher, Sergei set to work on drawing the diagrams. We decided that hand-drawn origami diagrams had a much friendlier look than computer-generated pictures, and Sergei is an accomplished draftsman. I would receive E-mail messages from Sergei containing phrases like, "I am machine gun!" You could almost hear him panting as he rushed to draw as many pictures as he could every night. Within two months he was done, and sent his exquisite drawings to me in the post.

This brought to me a very challenging problem. The easiest and most economical way of getting an origami book published is to produce the whole thing yourself on computer. That way your publisher can take your book on disk and give it to their printer, eliminating many tedious steps in the publishing process, saving time and money. This was the process I used in *Origami, Plain and Simple*, and I had agreed to submit *Russian Origami* on computer as well. Thus I began a long process of learning how to scan Sergei's wonderful pictures into my computer, without destroying the hand-drawn quality and without eating up all of my computer's memory. It was also my job to design the layout and compose the text. While Sergei knows English well enough to communicate in E-mail, his prose would have made my editor scream. Did this joint effort work? I think so, and you're holding our collaboration in your hands. As strange as it seems, Sergei and I have given birth to a book, without ever having met each other!

There are a number of interesting points of which the origami enthusiast should take note. All of these models are created by people who, in many ways, are out of the "origami loop." Russian paperfolders have a hard enough time communicating with each other, let alone with the origami organizations of Japan, America, and Europe! Thus while there are many classic bases that you see being used—the Preliminary Fold and the Pinwheel, Fish, and Waterbomb Bases—there are many things that you do *not* see. Only one model, the Matrioshka Doll, uses the sink procedure, and none of the models in this book start with the classic Bird Base, which is the foundation of so much origami in the West and Japan. At the same time, the style of these Russian models is very modern. Much Western origami from the sixties and seventies used multiple sheets of paper to reduce complexity, say, using two pieces of paper for the front and back of a horse. While several of the models in this book require more than one sheet of paper, they do so in efficient and creative ways, not merely as a short cut. As in recent Western styles,

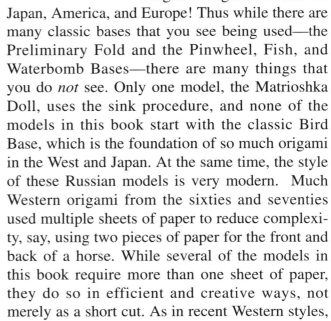

few crimps are used to add detail or character.

This book offers a rare opportunity to glimpse how origami traditions can develop in a culture isolated from our own, and to see how minds worlds away can often think alike. Indeed, a few of the models in this book are the product of simultaneous discovery! That is, some models, like Sergei Afonkin's Crown, were independently discovered by non-Russian paperfolders years ago. (This Crown was also discovered by the renowned Nick Robinson of England.) Such parallel discoveries are bound to happen in an art like origami and should be cause for marvel, rather than grounds for dispute.

I am sure that the innocent creativity of these Russian-created origami models will have a lasting impact on the worldwide origami community. Several, like Sergei's Flapping Dove and Zhenia Nikokosheva's Flower, are destined to become classics in the origami canon. Good, simple origami models are the most difficult to create, yet they leave the deepest impressions in the world of origami, since they are the easiest to teach and share.

The models in this book were chosen for their originality and simplicity. Thus *Russian Origami* should be viewed as a beginner-level origami book, although there is plenty of material here to entertain the most accomplished paperfolder. The instructions were drawn with the novice in mind. Pay attention to details, and you should have many hours of origami success!

In addition to the models, we have included brief biographies of the different Russian creators, as well as portraits whenever possible. Behind each model is a person (in many cases a Russian child!) who enjoys origami and has made it a part of his or her life. This book is as much about people as it is about origami.

I find the mere fact that this book exists to be an amazing thing. Growing up during the seventies and eighties, when the cold war showed no signs of ending, when the Soviet Union was commonly referred to as "The Evil Empire," when my classmates largely believed that we had a better chance of experiencing a nuclear winter than of reaching the year 2000, I find myself writing this preface with a sense of relief, hope, and brotherhood. I never would have guessed that origami would allow someone from Russia to become such a part of my life!

Ever since young Sadako began folding 1,000 cranes in her hospital bed in Hiroshima, origami has been a symbol of peace. After all these years, in its sharing and unpretentious way, origami still manages to make the world a smaller place. Perhaps by folding the models in this book, you too will feel closer to Russia.

—THOMAS HULL
Wakefield, Rhode Island 1997

The Mystery of Origami in Russia

Dear friends!

I hope I can begin this introduction in this way. In the last five years origami has helped me find many good friends in foreign countries (as well as my own) whose hands I can now shake and whose company I can share. During this time I've come to feel that all paperfolders are members of one big family and I am grateful for this chance to share the secret of Russian origami. In my opinion, up till now my country is the biggest secret in origami, as well as a mysterious phenomenon.

I have a double tale to tell. The first part is why origami did not fully exist in Russia before 1991, when the St. Petersburg Origami Center came into being. The second part is why paperfolding has become so popular now in Russia and is spreading so fast! Surely I can't provide exact answers, since I am neither a sociologist nor a historian. I can only tell my own story, with suggestions, and subjective assumptions which should be treated as the testimony of a witness.

To begin, it should be pointed out that origami was not in complete absence in Russia before 1991. Students of all Russian teaching colleges were given lessons on folding simple figures from paper to use in their classrooms. Also, in the late 1980s several articles with origami instructions were published by Victor Beskrovnyh (a biologist who now lives in Germany) in a very popular Russian magazine called *Family and School*. Some foreign origami books were also available at that time for Russian children, in particular *Origami* by Kawai and *Origami for the Connoisseur* by Kasahara and Takahama. However, in many ways these books did not really exist in Russia. To understand this paradox I need to explain something about the Soviet Union.

You have to know that in the USSR the usual practice of printing second editions of books did not exist. A book was only published once. For a very short time it would be available in bookshops and then disappear for years like a small stone in a big swamp. Of course, this practice could only exist in a state without real market relationships in the economy. Nobody wanted to know the fate of a book when it was published. Wonderful success or failure, it did not matter.

Another thing needs to be taken into consideration. The origami books mentioned above were not published in the Soviet Union. They were among a small number of foreign books that the state bought every year. This was the single narrow stream of literature that trickled into my country from abroad. Of course the number of such books bought by the state was very limited. At that time when I was a student I bought every good book I saw in the bookstores because they were so fleeting.

Thus it was impossible to buy or receive other foreign origami books. Do not forget about the so-called Iron Curtain and the fact that in those days correspondence with strangers was very suspicious and foreign parcels were the evidence of a spy's intentions. Unfortunately it is only half a joke. Remember the novel *1984* by George Orwell.

You might be wondering why some Russian author didn't write his or her own origami book at that time. The lack of appropriate information is a serious hindrance to the art, but what about natural Russian skill and talent? The problem was that there were not very many publishing companies and houses in the Soviet Union. They could be easily counted. Among them only a few would publish craft books intended for families—books that children and their parents could enjoy together. I knew of four, maybe five. The circulation of these books was enormous. A single print run might consist of up to a million copies. This was normal. The state published books for its citizens. Do you know how many people live in Russia?

Thus the number of authors was very limited. Writers were very special people, either those whose talent was already acknowledged by communist bureaucrats or the bureaucrats themselves. It was a question of ideology, as well as of money. Big money. Enormous money.

A friend of mine, a very good painter who professionally illustrates books, told me that in 1984 he did one book and made enough money to live on for two years. He was no idler and soon worked on another book. Now, in the new market economy he illustrates three or four books a year just not to die of hunger. Ah, capitalism!

So when I told my friend, during the time of the Soviet Union, that I wanted to write and publish a biological book for children, he said that I was crazy. I was told that it was easier to have a cup of tea with the British Queen than to become an author in the Soviet Union. At that time, he was right. But times change. Unfortunately I have yet to receive an invitation to take tea with Her Majesty the Queen, but some Russian origami books have been published.

As far as I know, in most countries paperfolding is a private activity. For example, OrigamiUSA is a large and very good organization, something like a club where you can share information and make friends. It is independent of the state or the President of the United States or Congress. The situation was quite different in my country several years ago. Only those ideas and movements that were supported by the state had a chance to develop. Otherwise they went underground.

In 1991 when the idea to create a Russian Origami Center came into our minds we tried to find some state support. Surely it was a crazy idea and in vain. The last thing the agonizing Red Empire wanted was to know how to fold paper. On the other hand, at that time reforms were taking place and it was possible to register some social organizations. Also, in 1993 the state lost its X-ray control over all publishers. Many new ones began to appear like mushrooms after a warm rain, and the old ones began to gasp without the state's financial support. In this situation the chance to publish an origami book increased tenfold. Thus, origami as a social and cultural

phenomenon did not exist in Russia before 1991 because the flowers of art grow badly in the stony ground of a totalitarian state. Only global changes made it possible, in my opinion.

It also helped that interest in paperfolding among Russians was certainly big enough. During the past five years our Center has received thousands of letters from all over the country saying, "Please help! I tried to find information about paperfolding without any success, and I heard that you could help!" Teachers in primary schools and kindergarten, parents, children, all sent letters asking us to mail them information about origami. Answering their excited letters, to use a vivid metaphor, was like putting a lighted match into a dry stack of straw!

It may seem like another paradox, but the hard economic times that post-Soviet Russia faced, and still faces actually helped origami to spread so fast. This is because it is one of the cheapest ways to teach handicrafts to children. No colored pencils, no textbooks, no rulers, no thick albums, nothing is needed but a piece of paper and a teacher who looks like a magician. At that time our Center began giving origami courses for grown-up people, and this helped many of them find new jobs as teachers.

For example an old Russian woman told me that during her whole life she worked in a military factory that produced supersecret atomic submarines. Of course, when the Red Empire crashed she lost her job. Now she gives origami lessons in a kindergarten, and she is absolutely happy. The only thing she regrets is that she hadn't started this new career sooner!

To tell the truth, writing replies to this endless stream of mail from Russians thirsty for origami, began to get monotonous. To help, we published a newspaper titled "Peace of Origami," which first appeared in 1993. It was very cheap and everybody could buy it each month at the biggest bookshop in St. Petersburg. In printing the newspaper we could communicate information about origami to several thousand people at once. Inflation and the increasing cost of paper killed our newspaper after one year.

Then came the time of books. It is very strange that our first origami book, *Tricks and Games with Paper* was published by a company that normally prints chemistry books! They usually print books titled *Synthesis of Some Fat Amino Acids on High Pressure in a Liquid Phase* or something like that. Very dull. (Sorry, I hope there are no chemists reading this!) But the changing times forced this publishing company to issue other books to make money. Origami became a gold mine for this purpose. During this change the old system of book distribution throughout the country was completely destroyed, and a new system began to grow like the root of a young tree. Now origami books rise to the surface all over the country and new letters arrive from readers.

Our Russian origami books have an international nature. By this I mean that they include both foreign and Russian-created models. The appearance of the latter has stimulated the first attempts of Russian paperfolders to create their own models. To determine whether or not these creations were original, many of them were sent to our Center. When the number of models broke the two hundred mark, we decided to create our own Russian origami database. Today it includes more than 1000 models and information about them—author, his/her address, year, time, level of difficulty, number of steps, and key words so that it is easy to catalogue and locate the model. In fact, all the models in the book you hold in your hands came from our database! The database works very well, and I hope with time it will contain thousands of models.

New situations require new decisions for further growth. We certainly need to welcome paperfolders throughout the whole country into our community. As you know, Russia is very big, and its size causes problems. This is another paradox of our life because it is easier to travel from St. Petersburg to London than to cross my native country from west to east. We can't organize national origami conventions like they have in America, England, and Europe, but we try anyway! Now each March we hold a Russian Origami Conference in St. Petersburg and try to attract as many paperfolders as possible.

The next possible step was to create a Russian origami magazine that could gather the latest news and introduce new names. As soon as this idea came to our minds the heavens helped us again when an editorial company in Moscow asked me to run the magazine. Now this magazine comes out every other month, with a color cover, and everybody in my country can order it at any post office. It is very cheap, and I hope that everyone who wants it can have it.

To mention a further development, my dream has been to make origami a subject in primary school. During the last four years I have been giving origami lessons in a school where I work, and I see how desired these lessons are for children. After some practice I and my wife, Elena, who gives origami lessons for adults, wrote an origami textbook for primary schools. It has been published in Moscow, and I hope its fate will be great!

I hope you enjoy the fruits of origami the Russian tree has borne. We welcome your comments, stories and thoughts, so please feel free to write to us at the following address:

193318 Russia
St. Petersburg
P.O. Box 377
Origami Center c/o Sergei Afonkin
or E-mail us at: sergei@origami.nit.spb.su
Thank you, and good luck!

—SERGEI AFONKIN
THOMAS HULL (editor)
St. Petersburg, Russia 1997

Folding Advice

The instructions in this book were drawn with the origami novice in mind. When learning origami from a book a person looks at a two-dimensional picture and somehow translates this into a three-dimensional movement of the hands. In a sense, the origami novice is trying to learn two things at the same time: (1) the rules of how paper can fold and (2) the language of origami diagram instructions! Keep the following advice in mind as you tackle the models in this book.

- For the most part, the models **start out easy**, and get progressively more difficult as you go through the book. So begin with the first models in the book and work your way up.

- When starting out, you might have an easier time if you fold on a **flat surface**, like a large book or a table.

- **Pay attention** to details! Every line in each picture is there for a reason. If your model doesn't look like the illustration, then you might have missed something, and should go back a step.

- If you don't understand what a symbol means, try looking at the **List of Symbols** in the Appendix. Or look for another model that uses the symbol, and see if you can figure out what it means there.

- When trying to figure out a certain step, **look ahead** to the next picture to see what the result is supposed to look like. This can be a BIG help!

- If you really get stuck, try asking a **friend** for help. Two minds are better than one!

Origami Paper

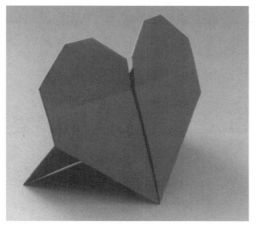

Special origami paper is a big help when trying to learn origami. This paper folds very well and is colored on one side and white on the other. It can be found in most art supply stores, or you can order it through OrigamiUSA, a not-for-profit organization devoted to spreading the word of origami. For a free catalogue as well as information about our organization, send a self-addressed, stamped envelope to:

OrigamiUSA
Box RO-1
15 West 77th Street
New York, NY 10024
USA

Bull's Head
by Sergei Afonkin

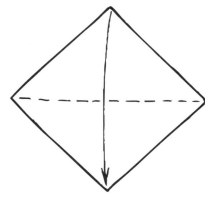

(1) White side up. Fold in half from corner to corner to make a triangle.

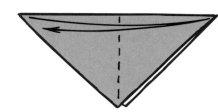

(2) Fold this triangle in half and unfold.

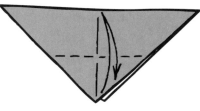

(3) Then fold **one layer** of the bottom point up to the middle of the top edge and unfold.

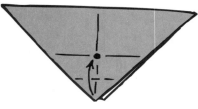

(4) See where the two previous creases intersect? Fold the bottom corner up to that point.

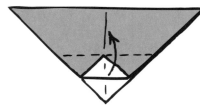

(5) Then refold the crease from step 3.

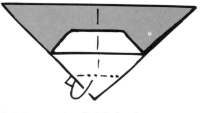

(6) Mountain-fold the bottom point behind.

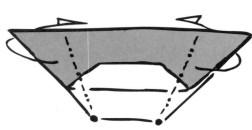

(7) Now mountain-fold the left and right sides behind to make horns!

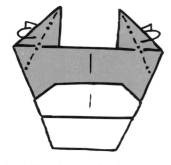

(8) Slim down the horns . . .

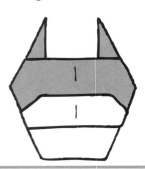

(9) . . . and you're done! Drawing a face will add character to your Bull's Head.

Two Swans
by Galina Skorohvatova

This simple, elegant swan of Galina's has the amazing quality of being closely related to other swans in the origami canon while at the same time bearing an unmistakable stamp of originality!

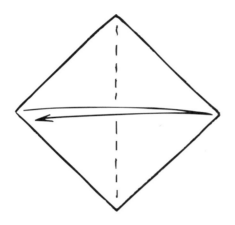

(1) White side up. Fold and unfold a diagonal.

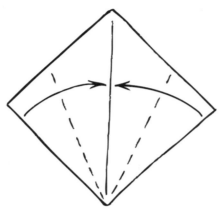

(2) Then fold the bottom sides to the center line, to make a cone.

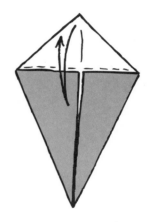

(3) Fold the top point down and unfold.

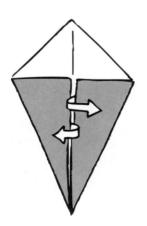

(4) Open everything up again.

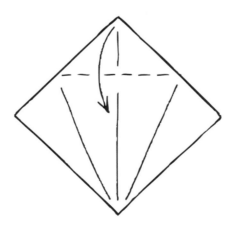

(5) Refold the crease from step 3.

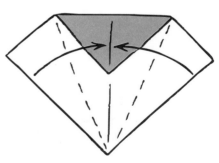

(6) Then refold the creases from step 2!

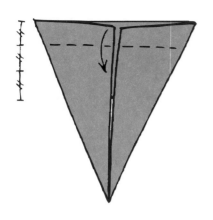

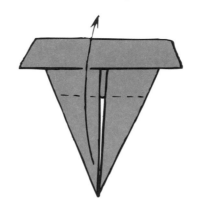

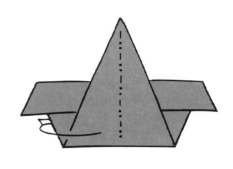

(7) OK! Fold the top edge down.

(8) Now see the corner of paper hiding inside the model? Fold the bottom point up so that the crease lies on this corner.

(9) Mountain-fold in half away from you.

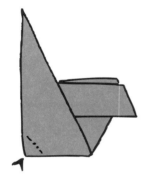

(10) Is it starting to look like a swan? Push the bottom corner inside.

(11) Fold the top corner down at an angle . . .

(12) . . . like this. (Enlarged view!) Make this crease **firm** and unfold.

(13) Now use the creases that you just made to **reverse** the point. The result will be the swan's head.

(14) See? The swan now has a head! Return to normal view.

(15) Hold the model at the indicated spots and pull the neck forward a little. Then flatten the model.

To Make a Sleeping Swan

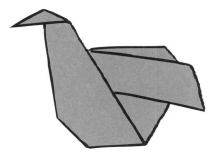

(16) The completed Swan!

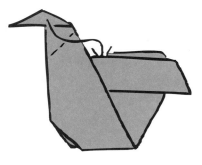

(1) Fold the neck to the right and tuck the beak in between the wings.

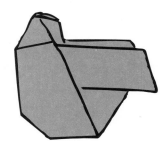

(2) A sleeping swan!

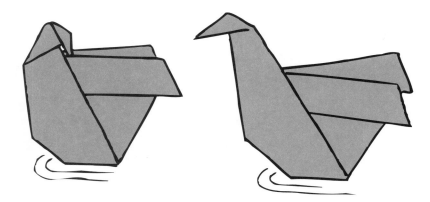

About the Creator

What is the most important feature of successful origami? The level of complexity? Not at all! Many paperfolders would argue that fresh perception of living objects is more important. The artist needs to be able to take an object from the world, distill it into its simplest elements and then capture these in a folded sheet of paper. This process of abstraction requires quite a bit of artistic intuition, and young Galina, after attending origami lessons in her school for two years, seems quite adept at it. Galina's swans are very simple models, yet in spite of that simplicity you can almost see two live birds swimming on still water!

Galina Skorohvatova

Hat
by Igor Kassihin

This amazingly simple hat is closely related to other origami hats that one finds in the Western and Japanese traditions, but has a unique character that is Russian all the same.

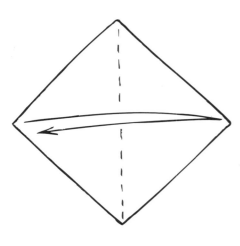

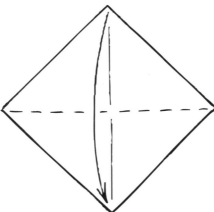

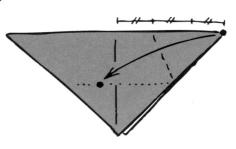

(1) White side up. Fold and unfold a diagonal.

(2) Then fold the top corner to the bottom. (The other diagonal.)

(3) Fold the right corner to the left, so that its lower edge is horizontal.

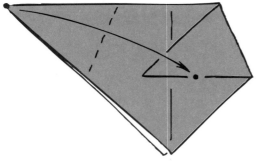

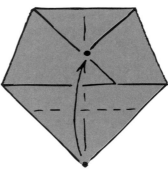

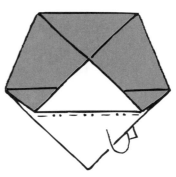

(4) Do the same thing with the left corner.

(5) Then fold up **one layer** to the indicated point.

(6) Mountain-fold the other layer behind by the same amount.

 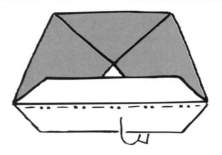 

(7) Fold a flap up . . .   (8) . . . and do the same thing behind.   (9) Finally, open up the hat. Push in on the sides and top to make the hat stay open.

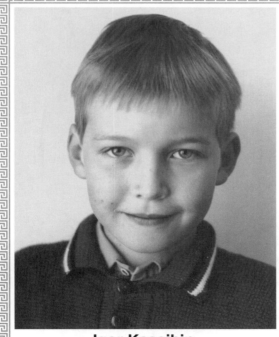

(10) The completed Hat! If you start with a 20-inch square you'll get a hat that will fit a big head.

About the Creator

Igor's father teaches Spanish in a school where origami is taught in the first grade. He wrote about his son's enthusiasm for paperfolding: "For a while origami substituted all other games and amusements for my son. His mother was in a panic—how can you clean a flat where each corner is full of paper birds and dinosaurs? But surely we are glad this has happened because we never had to force Igor to fold something. All by himself he studies every origami model in every detail! Due to his enthusiasm we have seen how beautiful this wonderful world of origami is!"

Igor Kassihin

Crown
by Sergei Afonkin

For this model you must make four identical pieces and then put them together to form the crown! This was independently created by British paper-folder Nick Robinson.

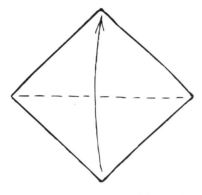

(1) White side up. Fold the bottom corner to the top to make a triangle.

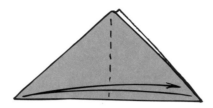

(2) Fold this triangle in half and unfold.

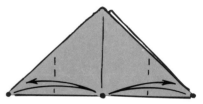

(3) Then fold the left and right corners to the center and unfold.

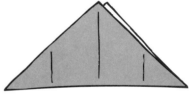

(4) Done with one piece of the crown! Make 3 more such pieces.

To Make the Crown

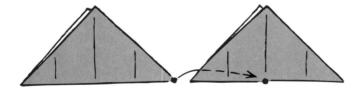

(1) Slide one unit half-way into another unit . . .

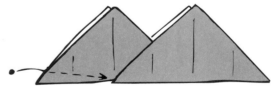

(2) . . . like this! Then slide in a third unit, and then the fourth.

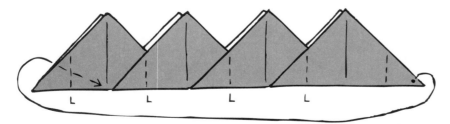

(3) After the fourth piece is in place, wrap the whole thing around to slide the first one into the last.

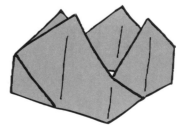

(4) The completed Crown, ready for wearing!

Ornament 1
by Anton Vuima

This modular ring requires eight squares of paper. It makes a great Christmas ornament!

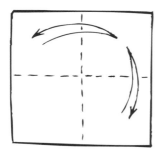

(1) White side up. Fold and unfold the diagonals.

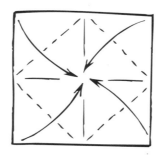

(2) Then **blintz**! That is, fold all four corners to the center.

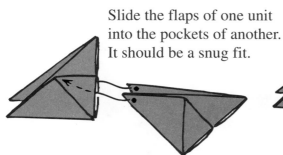

(3) Fold the bottom point to the top to make a triangle.

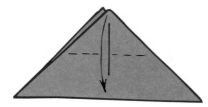

(4) (Enlarged view.) Fold one flap down to the bottom edge.

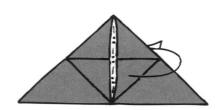

(5) Mountain-fold in half away from you.

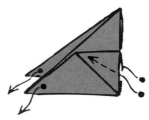

(6) You're done with one unit! Now make 7 more. Notice where the flaps and pockets are.

How to Put Them Together

Slide the flaps of one unit into the pockets of another. It should be a snug fit.

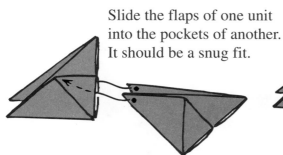

Continue with the other units.

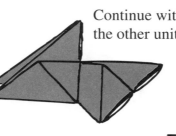

The completed Ornament!

About the Creator

Anton is a student who is training to be a professional musician. His father is an architect, and perhaps this influence is why Anton began making his own constructions with paper. Anton says that he likes the geometry of folded paper. It's a pleasure for him to see how modules fit exactly into each other to make beautiful ornaments!

Ornament 2
by Max Efremov

This modular ring requires ten squares of paper. That might seem like a lot, but each unit only takes seven steps. Try it!

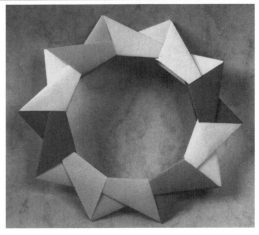

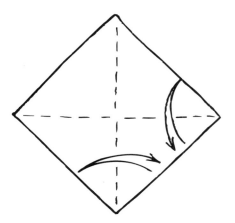

(1) White side up. Fold and unfold both diagonals.

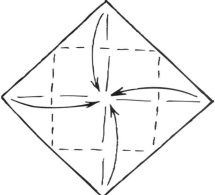

(2) Then blintz. That is, fold all four corners to the center.

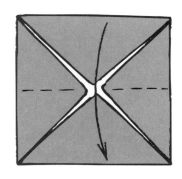

(3) (Enlarged view.) Fold the top to the bottom.

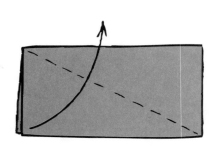

(4) Then fold the left corner up, front layer only. **Pay attention**, though, to how the crease is supposed to hit the upper left and lower right corners.

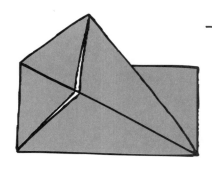

(5) Cool, eh? Turn over.

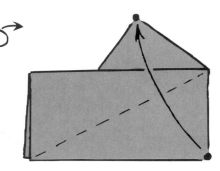

(6) Do the same thing on this side; fold the lower right corner up to meet the other one.

How to Put the Units Together

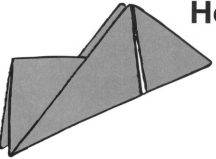

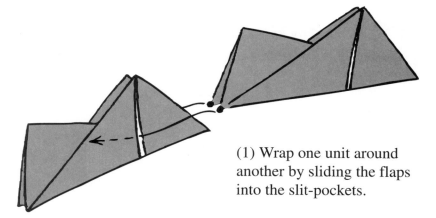

(7) The completed unit. Now make 9 more!

(1) Wrap one unit around another by sliding the flaps into the slit-pockets.

About the Creator

Unlike the mined rivers of Colorado, the origami river is still full of gold nuggets. Just playing with paper will sometimes lead one to gems that are simple yet very interesting. But few explorers wander across the valleys of this river. Max Efremov, who lives in Moscow, is one such explorer, and has found some gold of his own. He hopes that you might also discover some treasures during your own explorations!

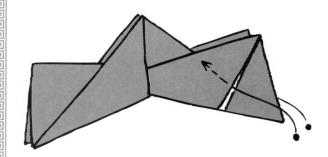

(2) Then slide another one in, and another, to make a ring. Be careful to hold them together before the last one is in place!

Max Efremov, in his bedroom

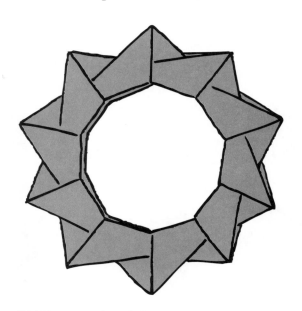

(3) The completed Ornament! Make one with pretty colors and hang it in your home.

Stars

by Tania Shahova

This 8-unit star has two variations.

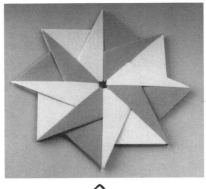

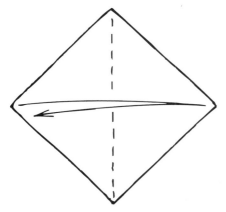

(1) White side up. Fold and unfold a diagonal.

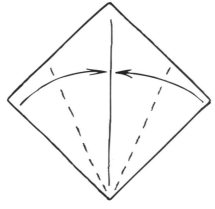

(2) Then fold the bottom sides to the center line, to make a cone.

(3) Fold the top point down.

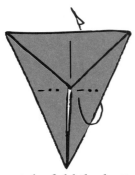

(4) Mountain-fold the bottom point away from you. Make the crease flush with the tip of the flap from step 3.

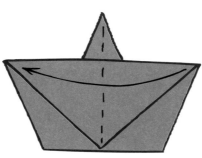

(5) Fold in half . . .

(6) . . . and you're done! Make 7 more.

Putting the Units Together

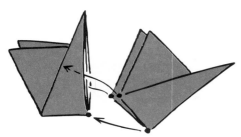

(1) Insert the bottom left corners of one unit into the white pockets of another . . .

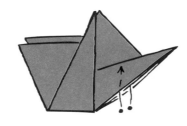

(2) . . . like this. Then insert another one, and another, and so on.

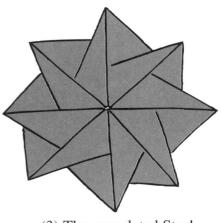

(3) The completed Star!

A star variation

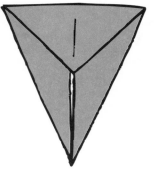

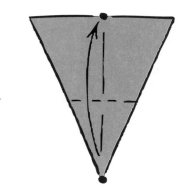

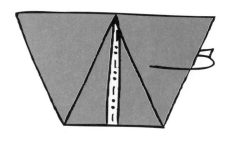

(1) Start with step 4 of the previous star. Turn over.

(2) Fold the bottom point to the top.

(3) Mountain-fold in half away from you.

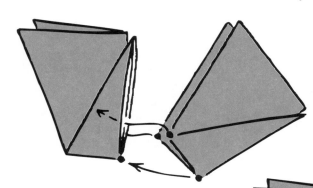

These units go together in the same way as the previous ones.

(4) Done with one unit! Can you see the difference between this one and the previous star? Make 7 more.

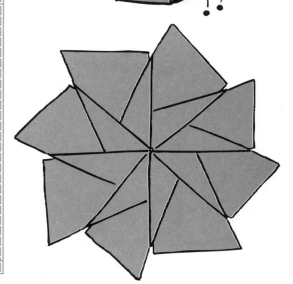

About the Creator

Tania is a mathematics schoolteacher. Some Russian math teachers, including Tania, try to combine mathematics, geometry, and origami. One can describe over and over to students what an angle bisector is, but it is much easier to have them fold an angle in half and see what it is at once! In this way origami makes some mathematical and geometrical concepts clearer, especially for students who are visually or artistically inclined. It is interesting to note that such approaches to teaching math with paperfolding are also taking place in American classrooms.

A different Star! Can you come up with other variations?

Four-Point Star

by Sergei Afonkin

This modular star only requires four squares of paper.

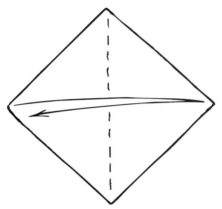

(1) White side up. Fold and unfold a diagonal.

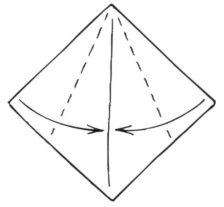

(2) Then fold the top sides to the center line, to make a cone.

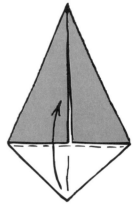

(3) Fold the bottom point up.

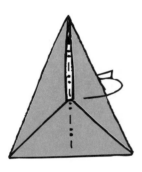

(4) Mountain-fold in half away from you.

(5) Now fold the lower right corner up to the left. Make the crease flush with the cut edge of the paper.

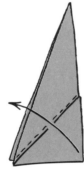

(6) Unfold.

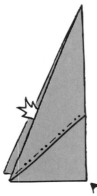

(7) Then reverse-fold the lower right corner through . . .

(8) . . . like this. Done! Make 3 more.

Putting the Units Together

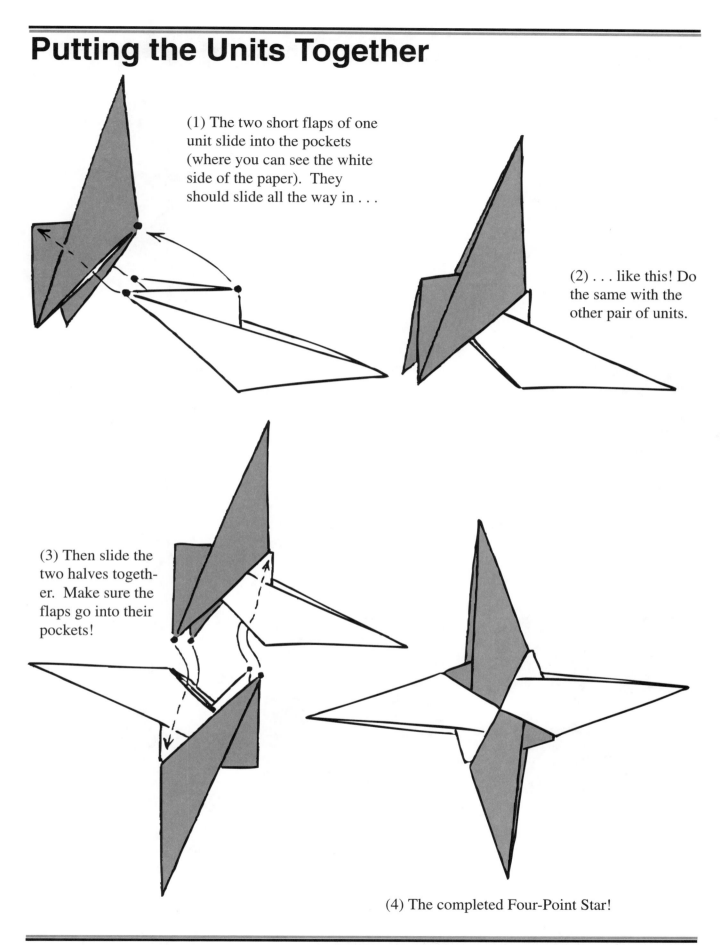

(1) The two short flaps of one unit slide into the pockets (where you can see the white side of the paper). They should slide all the way in . . .

(2) . . . like this! Do the same with the other pair of units.

(3) Then slide the two halves together. Make sure the flaps go into their pockets!

(4) The completed Four-Point Star!

Flower

by Zhenia Nikokosheva

This incredibly elegant, yet simple flower is made from two sheets of paper, one for the flower and one for the stem.

The Flower

The instructions below will produce a white flower. To make a colored flower start with the colored side up.

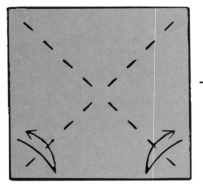

(1) Fold and unfold both diagonals. Turn over.

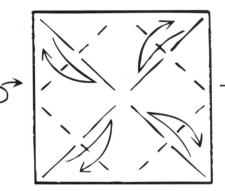

(2) Then fold the four corners to the center. Unfold and turn over again!

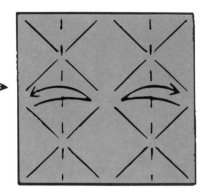

(3) Fold and unfold the left and right sides to the center.

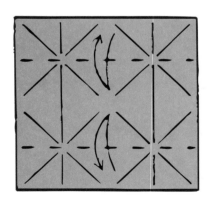

(4) Fold and unfold the top and bottom edges to the center.

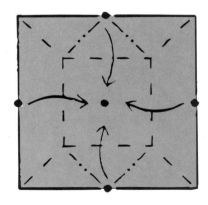

(5) OK! Now bring the center points of the top and bottom edges to the center of the square and collapse . . .

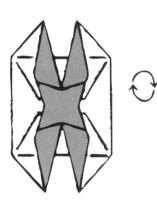

(6) . . . like this! Make sure the diagonal creases at the corners are being used. Collapse it flat and rotate 90°.

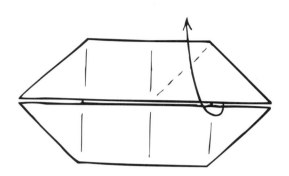

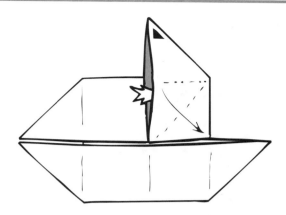

(7) Yeah! You've just folded what is sometimes called the Pinwheel Base. Now fold the upper right corner upward.

(8) Open the pocket and flatten it down toward the center; watch the black triangle.

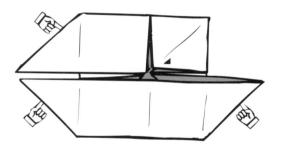

(9) Then repeat steps 7 and 8 on the other three flaps.

(10) Fold each of the four center flaps to the outer corners.

(11) See the four flaps in the center that were hidden in the previous step? Fold each of them to the side and unfold.

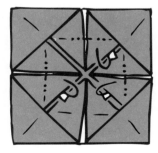

(12) Now mountain-fold three of those flaps **behind**, into the model. (You'll use the creases we just made.)

(13) All right! We're done with the flower part of the model. Put this aside and get another square of paper for the stem.

The Stem

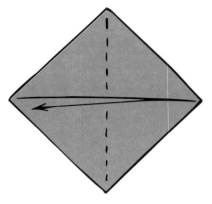

(1) White side up. Fold and unfold along one diagonal.

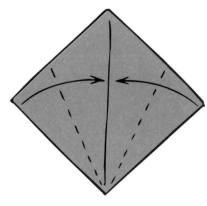

(2) Fold the two lower sides to the center. (This is called an ice-cream cone fold.)

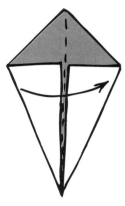

(3) Fold the whole thing in half.

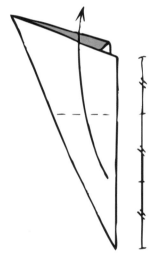

(4) Fold the bottom point up at a point approximately a third of the way down, as shown. **Crease firmly**!

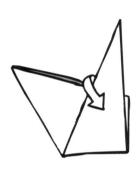

(5) Unfold step 4.

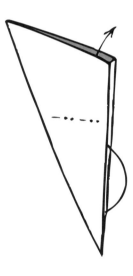

(6) Now use the creases you just made to reverse-fold the point up through the model. This forms the stem.

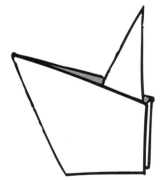

(7) Done with the stem! All you have to do now is put the flower on the stem. Read on.

Putting the Flower and Stem Together

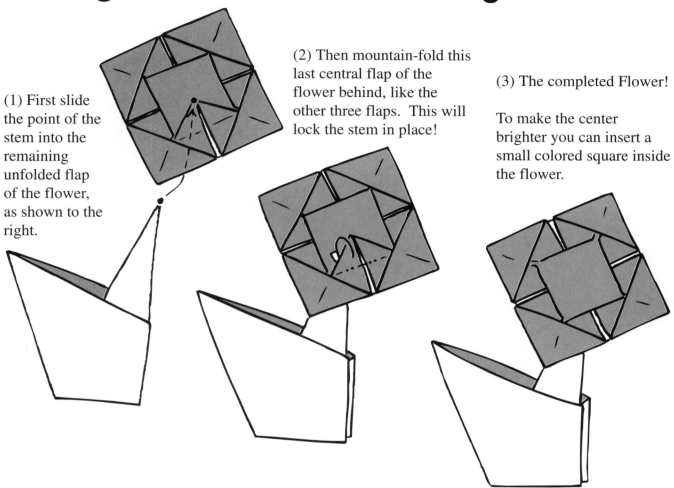

(1) First slide the point of the stem into the remaining unfolded flap of the flower, as shown to the right.

(2) Then mountain-fold this last central flap of the flower behind, like the other three flaps. This will lock the stem in place!

(3) The completed Flower!

To make the center brighter you can insert a small colored square inside the flower.

Zhenia Nikokosheva

About the Creator

Children are very good creators, perhaps because they haven't yet had the time to absorb all the limits of the grown-up world. This model is a perfect example. Eight-year-old Zhenia quickly invented this beautiful flower after an origami lesson in her school. She had no idea that the two pieces used in her model are very well-known in the origami world, but until Zhenia no one had thought to put them together in this way. To her it was a natural combination!

Mushroom

by Sergei Afonkin

In order to get the correct proportions for this mushroom, some unusual folding steps have to be made first. Pay attention to the details and you'll do fine!

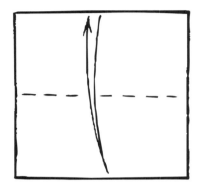

(1) White side up. Fold the bottom edge to the top and unfold.

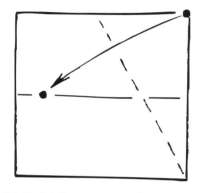

(2) Fold the upper right corner to the horizontal crease, making sure your fold goes through the lower right corner . . .

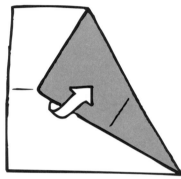

(3) . . . like this. Notice how the fold goes through the lower right corner? Unfold.

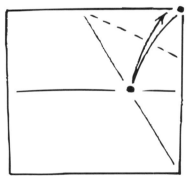

(4) See where the two previous creases intersect? Fold the upper right corner to that point and unfold.

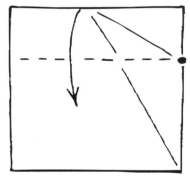

(5) Now fold top edge down, using the landmark to the right as a guide.

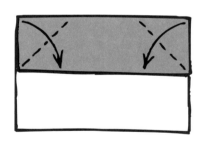

(6) Then fold the two top corners down.

(7) Unfold step 6.

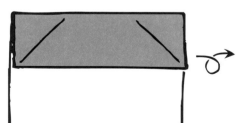

(8) Turn over.

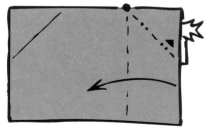

(9) Now fold the right side over, opening the layer underneath as you do so; watch the black triangle.

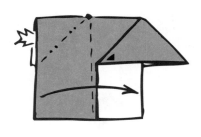 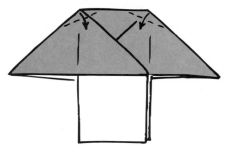 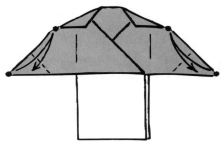

(10) Then do the same thing to the left side. You should start to see the mushroom take form!

(11) Round the top of the 'shroom by folding in the top corners.

(12) Fold and unfold the left and right corners as shown.

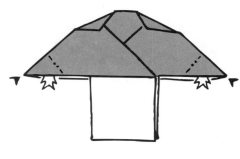 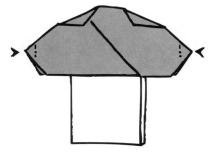 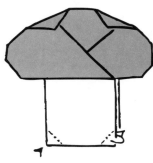

(13) Now **reverse-fold** the left and right corners inside. (This will use the creases made in step 12.)

(14) Round the sides even more by reverse-folding inward the left and right points.

(15) Now round the base of the mushroom with a reverse fold on the left and a mountain fold on the right.

 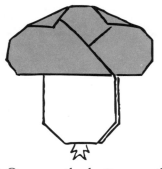 

(16) Then reverse-fold the remaining lower right corner to finish rounding off the bottom.

(17) Open up the bottom so the mushroom can stand and turn over.

(18) The completed Mushroom!

Tyrolean Hat
by Nikita Holin

This hat is modeled after musicians' hats from the German city of Tyrol. They are often worn with a feather.

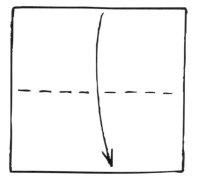

(1) White side up. Fold the top edge to the bottom.

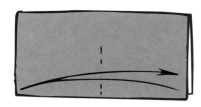

(2) Then pinch the half-way mark on the bottom. (The crease doesn't need to go all the way up.)

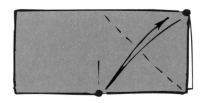

(3) Fold and unfold the upper right corner to the bottom center.

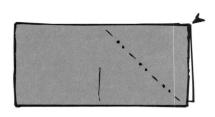

(4) Then, using the creases from step 3, **reverse-fold** the upper right corner inside.

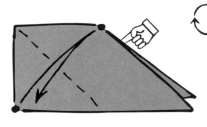

(5) Good! Now fold and unfold the bottom left corner. **Repeat behind**. Then rotate the model.

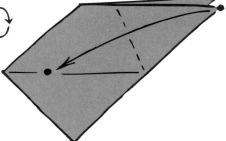

(6) Fold one of the rightmost points to the crease line that you just made.

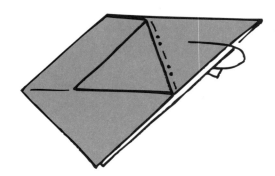

(7) Repeat step 6 on the other flap.

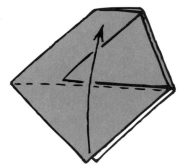

(8) Fold a single layer up.

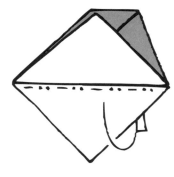

(9) Repeat step 8 behind.

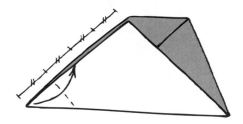 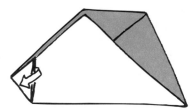 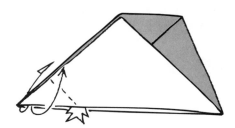

(10) Fold the lower left corner to halfway up the sloping edge.

(11) Then unfold!

(12) Now use the creases just made to make an outside reverse fold. It's like flipping up the visor on a baseball cap.

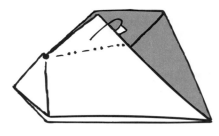 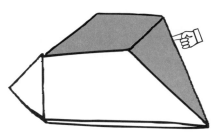 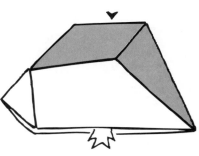

(13) The result should look like this! Tuck the excess white paper inside.

(14) Repeat step 13 behind.

(15) Now open up the bottom of the hat and push the top in a little to keep it open.

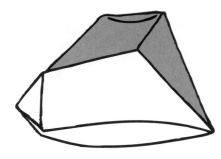 

The completed Tyrolean Hat! The feather is optional.

About the Model's History

This simple origami hat of Nikita's was inspired by the first Russian origami book, *Tricks and Games with Paper,* published in 1994 by a chemistry editorial company. During the Soviet Union this was a state-owned company that published very serious books devoted to different topics in chemistry. With the introduction of the free-market and the loss of state support, this company made a sharp turn towards publishing books for children and their parents. Origami was very suitable for this purpose, and some children who received such books began to create their own models.

Bell

by Sandra Afonkina

This simple bell can be strung and hung.

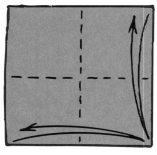

(1) Colored side up. Fold and unfold from side to side and from top to bottom. Turn over.

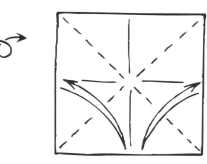

(2) Fold and unfold the diagonals.

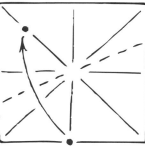

(3) Tricky: fold the bottom center up to the diagonal, but make sure the crease **goes through the center** of the square . . .

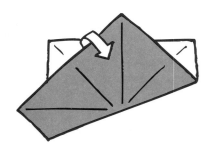

(4) . . . like this. See how the crease lines are all lined up? Unfold.

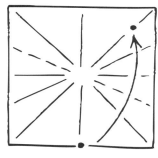

(5) Now repeat step 3, this time bringing the bottom center up to the other diagonal.

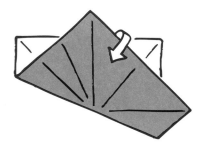

(6) Unfold.

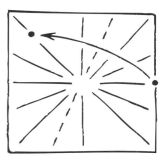

(7) Do step 3 again, but now fold the center of the right side to a diagonal . . .

(8) . . . like this. Unfold.

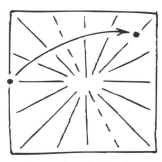

(9) One more time! See how all the creases go through the center? We will use them soon.

(10) Unfold.

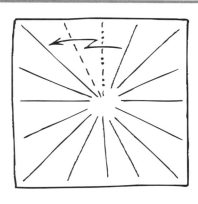

(11) OK! Now make a zig-zag pleat using two of the creases. The paper will become 3-D, like a bowl.

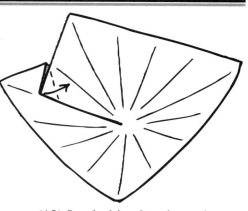

(12) Lock this pleat into place by folding the corner flap over.

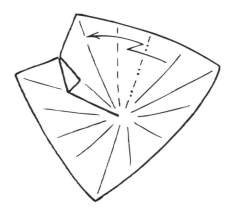

(13) Make another pleat . . .

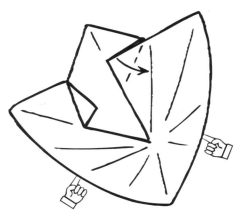

(14) . . . and lock this one in place too. Repeat this two more times and you're done with the Bell!

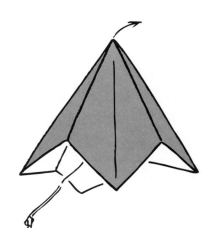

Thread a knotted string through the Bell to hang.

About the Creator

Sandra Afonkina

Sandra's first toys were the endless number of origami models folded by her paperfolding parents. Thus it was no big surprise when she began to fold her own models! When Sandra was thirteen she began giving origami lessons in her primary school. Now she has graduated from college and wants to be a teacher for disabled children. She dreams of using origami as a powerful method to teach spelling and other areas of learning.

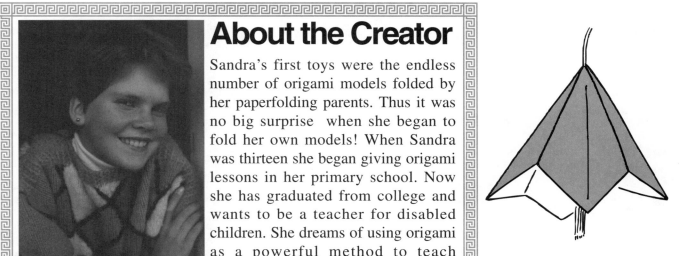

The completed Bell!

Russian Star
by Sergei Afonkin

Folding a five-pointed star has always been a challenge in origami, probably because the angles required can be difficult to produce. This model solves the problem by using a 2x1 sheet of paper.

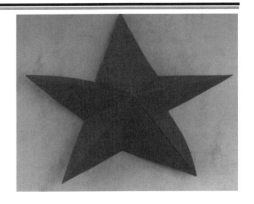

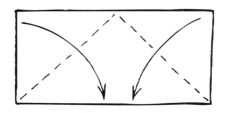

(1) White side up. Fold the top corners down to the center.

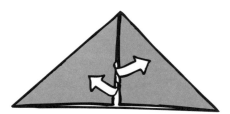

(2) Unfold.

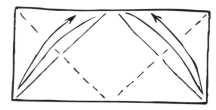

(3) Then fold and unfold the other diagonals.

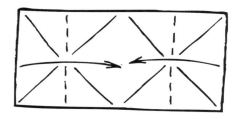

(4) Fold the sides to the center.

(5) Unfold. Then turn over.

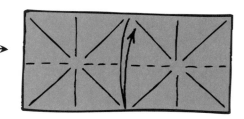

(6) Fold and unfold the bottom to the top.

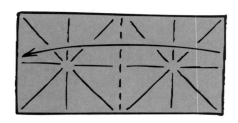

(7) Now fold in half from right to left.

(8) Fold the bottom right corner to the center.

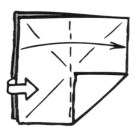

(9) Then fold one layer to the right.

(10) Mountain-fold the other layer behind.

(11) OK! Now use the existing creases to reverse-fold one of the upper left corners inside . . .

(12) . . . like this. Do the same thing to the other corner.

(13) Now reverse-fold the bottom left corner inside as well. This one is thicker. Let the inside layers go along for the ride.

(14) Then gently spread apart the layers to make a five-pointed star!

(15) The completed Russian Star!

Mouse Puppet

by Elena Anashkina

Create your own theatre with this origami finger puppet!

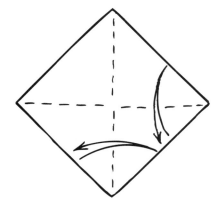

(1) White side up. Fold and unfold both diagonals.

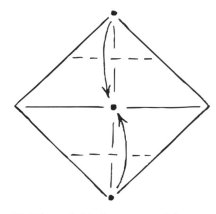

(2) Then fold the top and bottom points to the center.

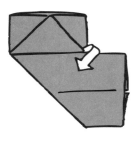

(3) Mountain-fold the left and right corners behind, to the center.

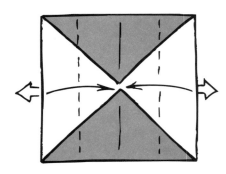

(4) Wow! Now fold the left and right edges to the center line, **but** let the flaps in back swing out . . .

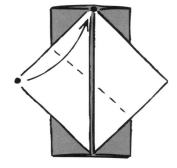

(5) . . . like this. Then fold the white square in half, as shown.

(6) Unfold!

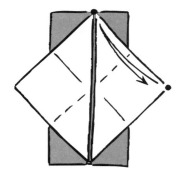

(7) Then do the same thing in the other direction.

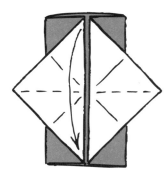

(8) Fold the top to the bottom.

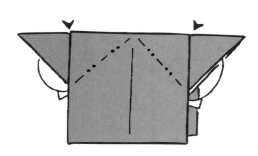

(9) OK. Now reverse-fold the two top corners inside. You'll use the creases made in steps 5 and 7.

 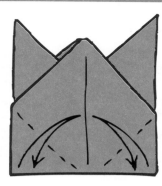 

(10) Then reverse-fold the corners back up to make mouse ears!

(11) Fold and unfold the bottom corners to the center. (Front layer only.)

(12) Now mountain-fold the bottom right corner, and tuck it into the pocket inside.

 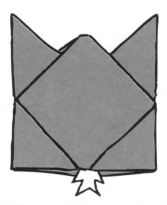 

(13) Tuck the left corner into the inside pocket as well.

(14) There will be a pocket for your finger to go into.

(15) Draw a face, and you're done with the Mouse Puppet!

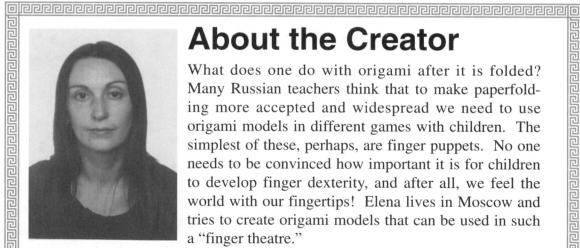

About the Creator

What does one do with origami after it is folded? Many Russian teachers think that to make paperfolding more accepted and widespread we need to use origami models in different games with children. The simplest of these, perhaps, are finger puppets. No one needs to be convinced how important it is for children to develop finger dexterity, and after all, we feel the world with our fingertips! Elena lives in Moscow and tries to create origami models that can be used in such a "finger theatre."

Elena Anashkina

Heart

by Elena Afonkina

This wonderful valentine is made from a 1 x 2 sheet of paper.

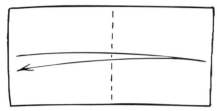

(1) White side up. Crease in half the long way.

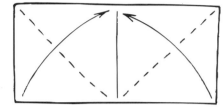

(2) Fold the bottom two corners to the top center.

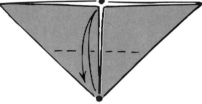

(3) Fold and unfold the bottom point to the top.

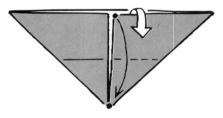

(4) Now, using the right half of the model, bring one layer down using the crease you just made.

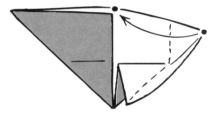

(5) (Step 4 in progress.) Flatten by bringing the right side to the center . . .

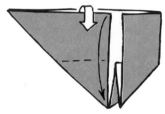

(6) . . . like this! Do the same thing on the left.

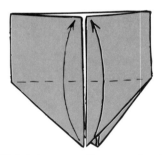

(7) Fold the two flaps at the bottom to the top.

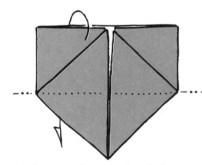

(8) Then swing the back layer down behind.

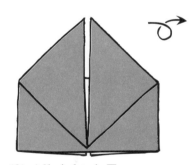

(9) All righty! Turn over.

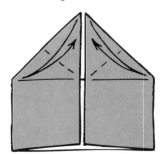

(10) Fold and unfold the top flaps to the side corners.

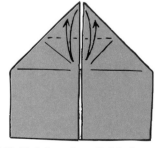

(11) Fold and unfold the top flaps to the center.

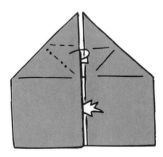

(12) Then open up the paper a bit to swivel part of the flap inside . . .

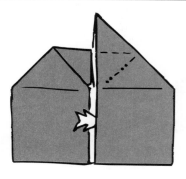 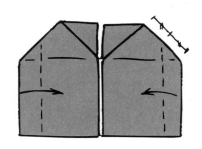 

(13) . . . like this. Repeat step 12 on the right.

(14) Fold the left and right sides in a bit.

(15) (Enlarged view!) Fold top corners to the folded edges.

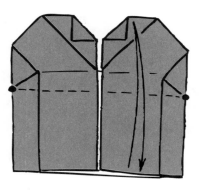 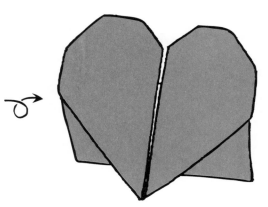 

(16) Fold the bottom flap up, crease sharply, and unfold. Turn over, and . . .

(17) . . . you're done with the Heart!

About the Creator

Elena is a midwife who works in a large, famous hospital in the center of St. Petersburg. In addition she teaches origami classes for adults, and during the past three years she taught almost two thousand students! As you can see in this book, Elena is the creator of many beautiful models. She has also been an unofficial (yet critical and valuable!) editor of every book written by her husband, Sergei. She studies psychology and dreams of investigating the effects of paperfolding in groups of young boys and girls.

Elena Afonkina

Clapping Monk
by Eugeni Fridryh

This is an action model; when you pull on the monk's head, the hands will clap!

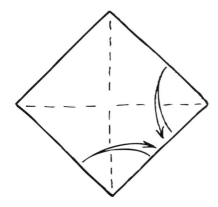

(1) White side up. Fold and unfold both diagonals.

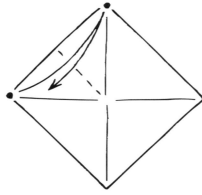

(2) Fold and unfold. **Notice** how the crease goes only to the center.

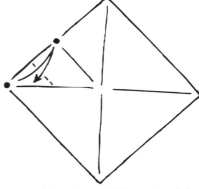

(3) Fold and unfold again; this time the crease you make is quite small.

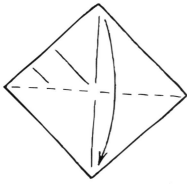

(4) Fold the top point to the bottom.

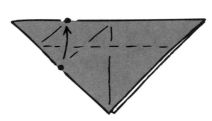

(5) Then fold one layer up. **Notice** the landmarks!

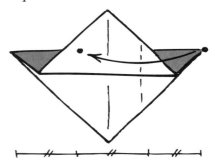

(6) Fold 1/3 of the way over.

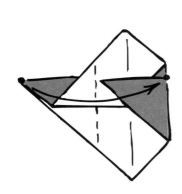

(7) Fold the left flap to the right.

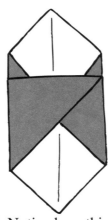

(8) Hey! Notice how things line up. (If they don't, you didn't do step 6 very accurately.) Turn over.

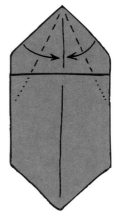

(9) Fold the top edges to the center line, allowing the paper to turn inside the model . . .

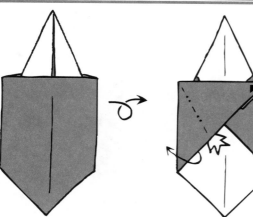 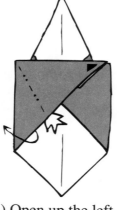 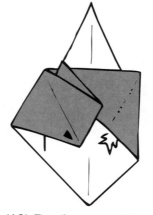 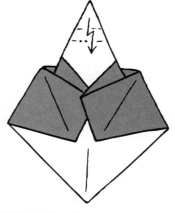

(10) . . . like this. Turn over.

(11) Open up the left flap and flatten it; watch the black triangle.

(12) Do the same thing to the right flap.

(13) Make the monk's hair by mountain-folding the top point down behind and then folding its tip up again.

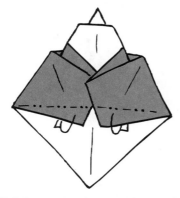 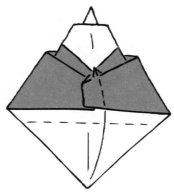 

(14) Mountain-fold some paper inside the model. (This forms the arms!)

(15) Lastly, fold the bottom point up inside the model, tucking it behind the white folded edge.

(16) The completed Monk!

About the Creator

What is more important for facilitating the spread of origami? Books? Creating lots of models? Good quality paper? No! It is people, people who share their enthusiasm with others. Eugeni is just this kind of person. During the past five years he was a student and thus often moved from place to place across the Siberia, the Eastern part of Russia. For example, in 1992 he lived in Tomsk, and now he teaches history in Novokusnetsk. But no matter where Eugeni lives he can soon be found surrounded by a cheerful flock of children, eager to learn origami models. With time Eugeni has become a more and more professional folder, to the point that now he teaches a course on origami at the East Art College.

How to Make the Monk Clap

Hold the base of the monk while pulling the head. The arms will clap, just like a real, live monk!

Flapping Dove
by Sergei Afonkin

Like the classic flapping bird, this elegant dove flaps its wings!

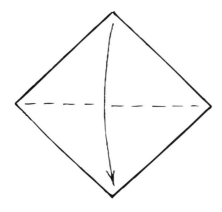

(1) Fold in half along a diagonal.

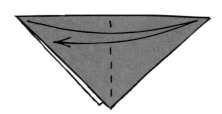

(2) Fold in half and unfold.

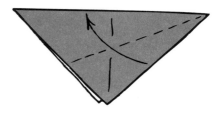

(3) Fold the side (**one layer!**) up to the diagonal.

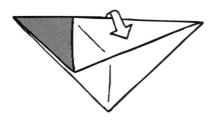

(4) Unfold step 3.

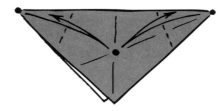

(5) See where the creases from step 2 and 3 intersect? Fold the left and right corners to this point and unfold.

(6) Fold the sides to the center line and unfold.

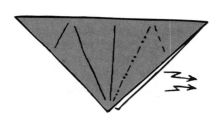

(7) OK. Now use the creases from the last two steps to crimp the right corner. It should zig in and zag out . . .

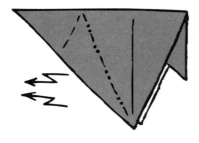

(8) . . . like this! (You had to change the direction of some of the creases, didn't you?) Do the same thing of the left.

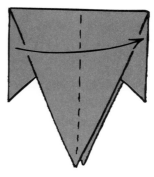

(9) Good! Now fold in half.

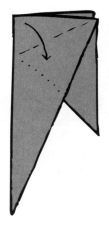

(10) Fold the top left corner down, using the X-ray line as a guide.

(11) Unfold step 10.

(12) Reverse-fold inside. This should "feel good."

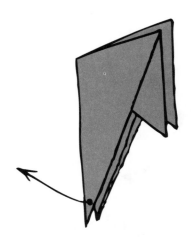
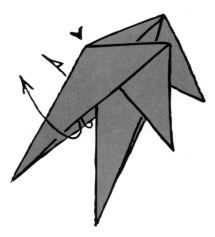
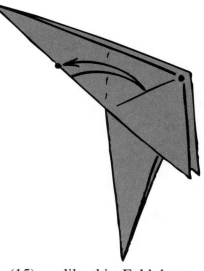

(13) Separate the two bottom points . . .

(14) . . . to open up the model and turn the left point inside-out . . .

(15) . . . like this. Fold dot to dot and unfold.

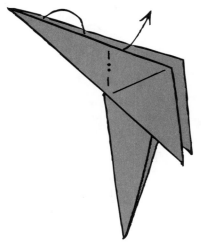

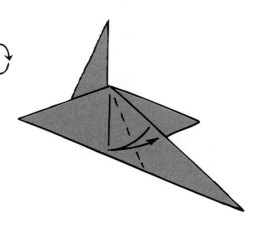

(16) Reverse-fold the point through, using the crease you just made.

(17) Can you start to see the dove? Fold one wing up and rotate a bit to the left.

(18) Fold the tail edge to the "center line" and unfold.

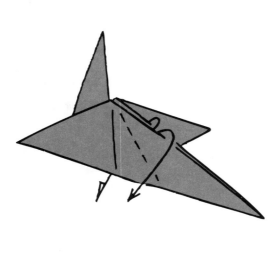

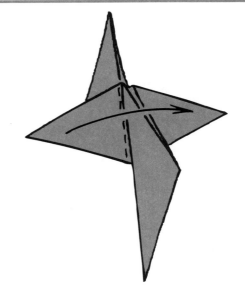

(19) Now use this crease to reverse-fold the tail down around the body.

(20) Yeah! Fold the wing back to the right.

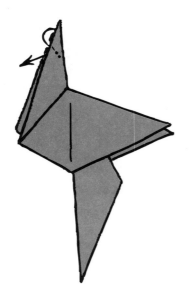

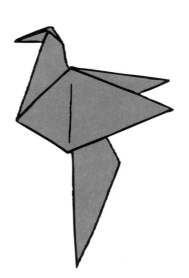

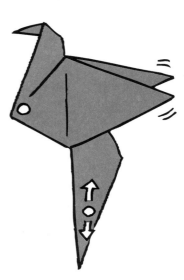

(21) Reverse-fold a head.

(22) Done with the Flapping Dove!

To make the dove flap, hold the breast and pull the tail.

Royal Crown
by Eugeni Fridryh

The long spires of this modular crown make it a very regal adornment. The basic unit is an interesting application of an off-centered Fish Base.

The Unit

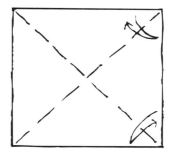

(1) White side up. Fold both diagonals and unfold.

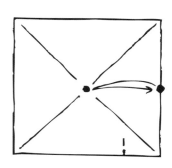

(2) Then bring the right edge to the center, but **only** pinch a crease at the bottom. Turn over.

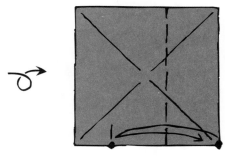

(3) Fold the right edge to the pinch mark made in the previous step. Unfold.

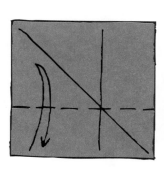

(4) Make a similar crease folding the bottom edge up, using the previous crease and the diagonal as a guide. Turn over and rotate the paper to the position shown in the next drawing.

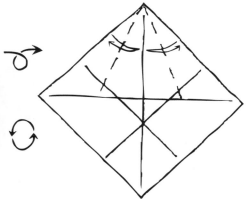

(5) Fold the top sides to the center diagonal, but **only** crease as far as the horizontal diagonal. Unfold.

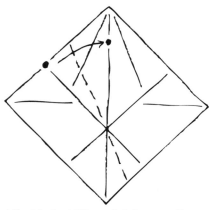

(6) Ah-ha! Now fold one of the creases from steps 3 or 4 to the center line . . .

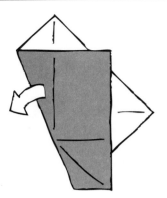

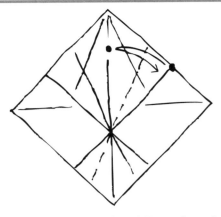

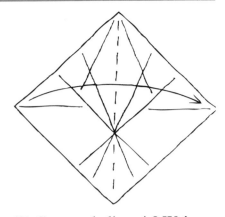

(7) . . . like this. Unfold.

(8) Repeat step 6 and 7 on the other side.

(9) Can you believe it? We're done with the precreasing! Fold in half from left to right.

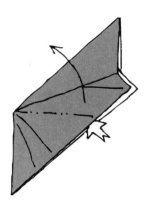

(10) Now use the crease lines to reverse-fold the top corner to the right.

(11) Fold one flap down in front and in back.

(12) Now open up the bottom and spread it flat . . .

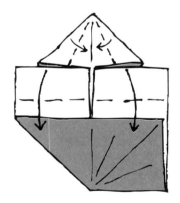

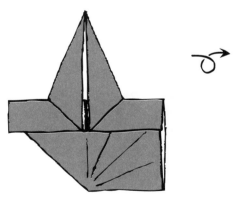

(13) . . . like this! Fold the white layers down—this will force the top corner to narrow . . .

(14) . . . like this. Turn over and you're done with one unit! Make as many as you want to make the Crown. You'll need at least 10.

How to Make the Royal Crown

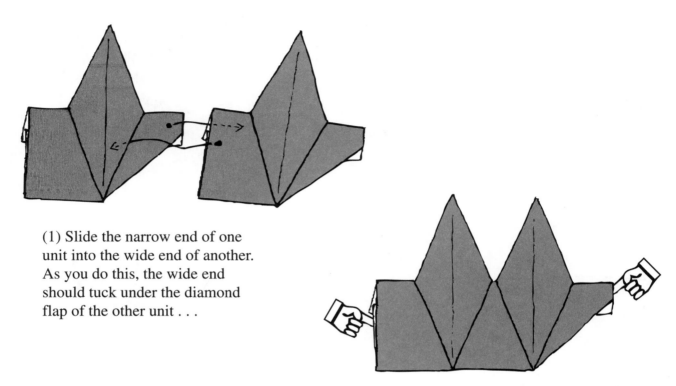

(1) Slide the narrow end of one unit into the wide end of another. As you do this, the wide end should tuck under the diamond flap of the other unit . . .

(2) . . . like this. Continue adding units to make a long strip. Then wrap it around to make the Crown.

(3) The completed Royal Crown, ideal for staking one's claim to the throne.

Christmas Star

by Sergei Afonkin

This four-piece modular star is another example of independent discovery by different cultures. The structure of the units closely resembles that of the "Stabile" model by American paperfolder Robert Neale.

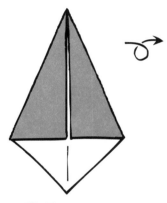

The Unit

The basic unit for this star is simply the classic Fish Base.

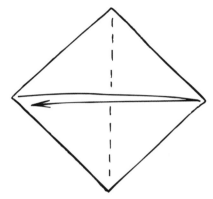

(1) White side up. Fold and unfold a diagonal.

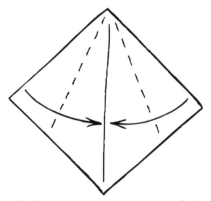

(2) Fold the upper edges of the square to the diagonal crease.

(3) Turn over.

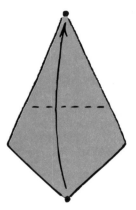

(4) Fold the bottom corner to the top.

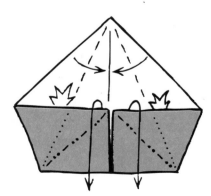

(5) OK! Now pull the inside flaps down. This will bring the sides of the paper together to make an inverted kite-shape . . .

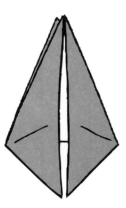

(6) . . . like this! Smooth it flat, and you're done with one unit! Make a total of 4.

Putting the Units Together

Interlocking the four units to make the Christmas Star is a complicated process. Pay attention!

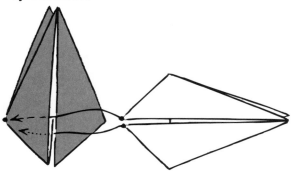 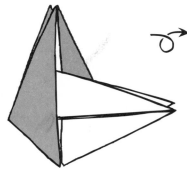 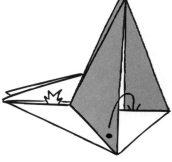

(1) Position two units as shown and slide the horizontal unit into the vertical one. The top point goes behind one layer of paper, into the pocket, while the bottom point goes behind two layers and sticks out the back.

(2) This is what you should see. Turn over from left to right.

(3) This is what the back should look like. Tuck the loose flap into the large pocket behind it.

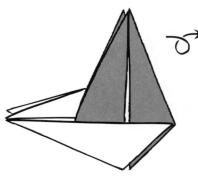 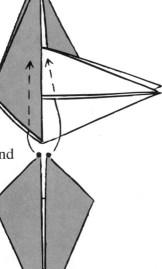

(4) OK! Turn over again and get another unit ready.

(5) Slip in the third unit, making sure that the left flap goes behind and the right one goes into the pocket.

(6) Turn over.

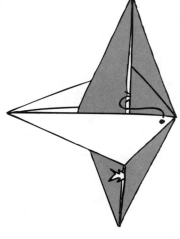 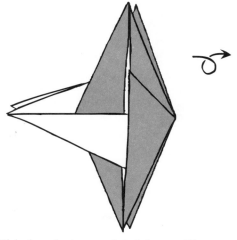

(7) Tuck the loose flap into the large pocket underneath.

(8) This is what you should see. Turn over and get ready for the last unit.

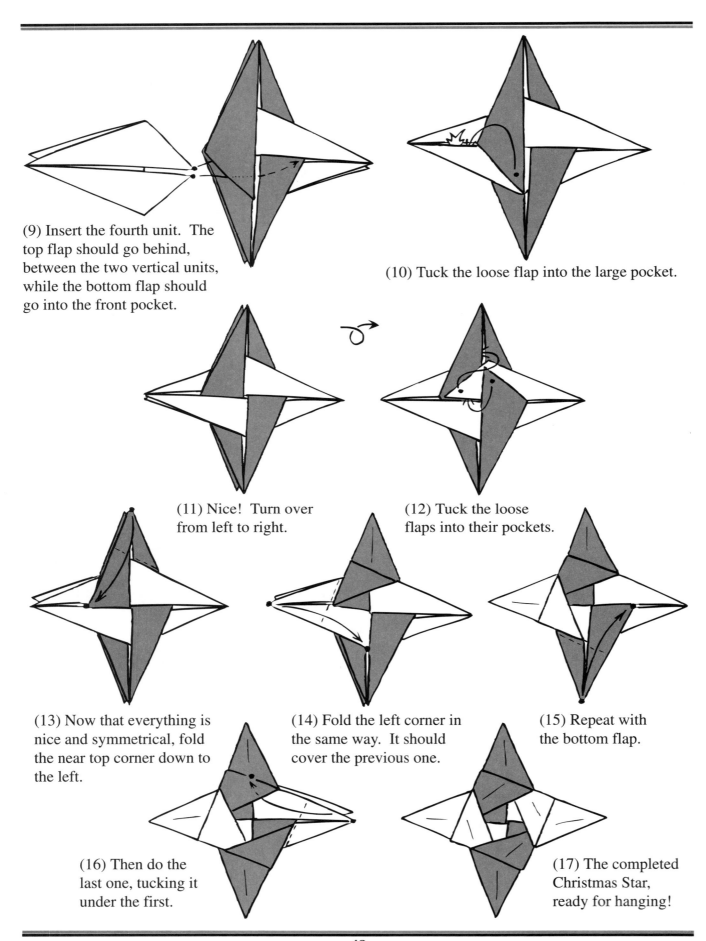

(9) Insert the fourth unit. The top flap should go behind, between the two vertical units, while the bottom flap should go into the front pocket.

(10) Tuck the loose flap into the large pocket.

(11) Nice! Turn over from left to right.

(12) Tuck the loose flaps into their pockets.

(13) Now that everything is nice and symmetrical, fold the near top corner down to the left.

(14) Fold the left corner in the same way. It should cover the previous one.

(15) Repeat with the bottom flap.

(16) Then do the last one, tucking it under the first.

(17) The completed Christmas Star, ready for hanging!

Two-Bases Star
by Sergei Afonkin

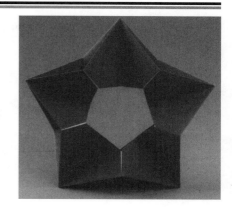

This modular star uses two of the fundamental origami starting points: the Preliminary Fold and the Waterbomb Base! The unit used in this model is the same used by Lewis Simon in his Gyroscope model.

The Preliminary Fold

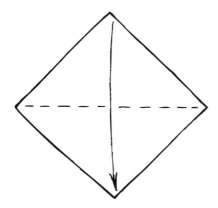

(1) White side up. Fold in half from corner to corner.

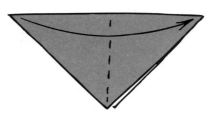

(2) Now bring the other two corners together and fold.

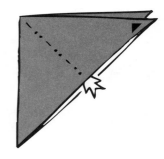

(3) Then open up one of the flaps and squash it flat into a square. Watch the black triangle.

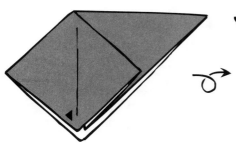

(4) Turn the paper over.

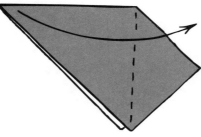

(5) Fold the left point to the right.

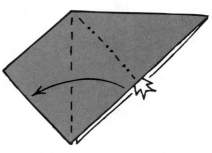

(6) Then repeat step 3 here—open up the flap and squash it flat.

Then you're done with the Preliminary Fold! This can be used to make many different origami models, and goes back to the classic Japanese origami tradition.

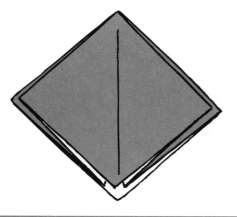

For the Two Bases Star model, you will need to make 5 of these Preliminary Folds.

The Waterbomb Base

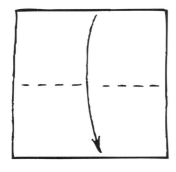

(1) White side up. Fold in half from top to bottom.

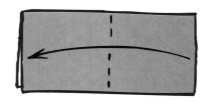

(2) Fold in half again.

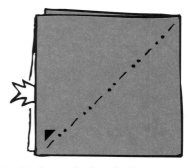

(3) (Enlarged view.) Open up one of the flaps and squash it flat into a triangle. Watch the black triangle.

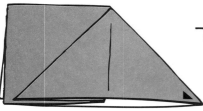

(4) Turn over.

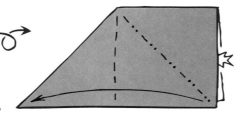

(5) Repeat step 3. That is, squash the flap into another triangle . . .

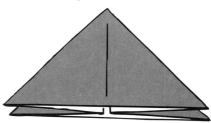

(6) . . . like this. The result is the classic Waterbomb Base! You'll need to make five for this model.

Creating the Two Bases Star

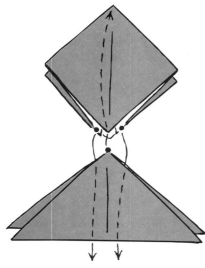

(1) Thread the two inner white points of the Preliminary Fold between the layers of the top of the Waterbomb Base. Slide the Waterbomb Base up as far as it will go.

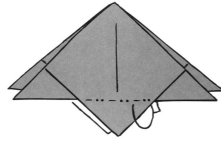

(2) Hook one of the flaps from the Preliminary Fold inside the Waterbomb Base.

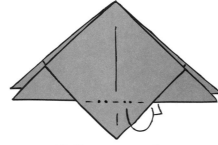

(4) Repeat step 2.

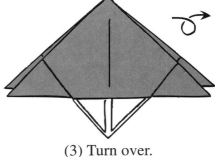

(3) Turn over.

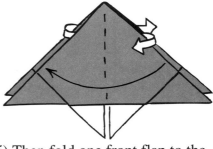

(5) Then fold one front flap to the left, and one back flap to the right.

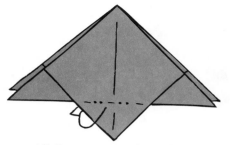

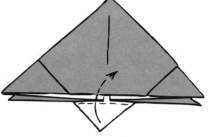

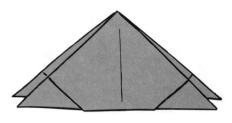

(6) Repeat step 2 again.

(7) Then tuck the last flap of the Preliminary Fold inside.

(8) Bingo! Now make 4 more using the remaining units.

Putting It All Together

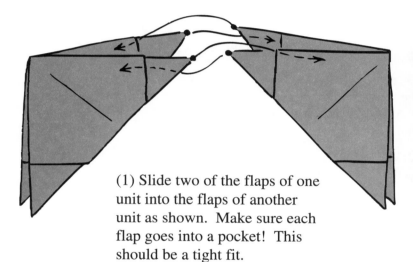

(1) Slide two of the flaps of one unit into the flaps of another unit as shown. Make sure each flap goes into a pocket! This should be a tight fit.

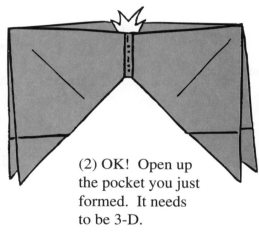

(2) OK! Open up the pocket you just formed. It needs to be 3-D.

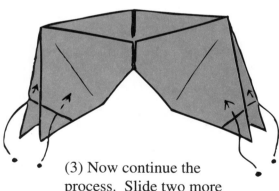

(3) Now continue the process. Slide two more units into the remaining two pairs of flaps. Then use the last unit to finish it up.

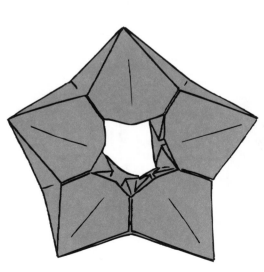

(4) The completed Two Bases Star!

Container

by Natalia Romashova

This model is made from a sheet paper cut to the European A4 proportion.

How to Make A4 Paper from a Square

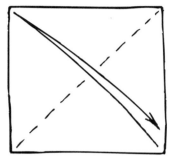

(1) Fold and unfold a diagonal.

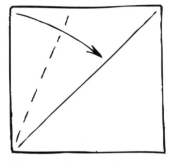

(2) Then fold the left edge to the diagonal.

(3) Unfold.

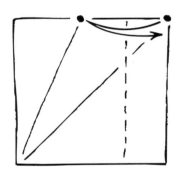

(4) Now fold the upper right corner to the point where the crease meets the top edge. Unfold.

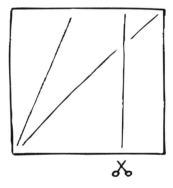

(5) Cut along this last crease, and you'll end up with a rectangle with proportions 1x $\sqrt{2}$. That's A4 size.

How to Make the Container

(1) White side up. Fold and unfold both diagonals. Turn over.

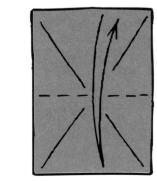

(2) Fold and unfold the top to the bottom. Turn over again!

(3) Now push the center in as you collapse the model . . .

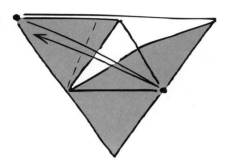

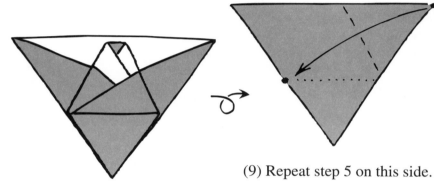

(4) . . . like this. Flatten and look at the model head-on.

(5) Fold one of the right corners to the midpoint of the left side.

(6) Fold the left corner similarly, and unfold.

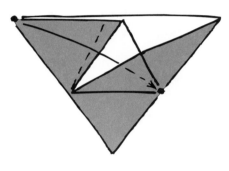

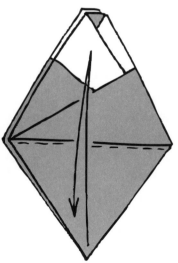

(7) Then refold step 6, but this time tuck the flap into the pocket.

(8) Neat, eh? Turn over.

(9) Repeat step 5 on this side.

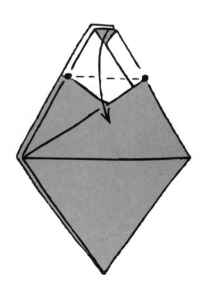

(10) Repeat steps 6 and 7 on this side too.

(11) (Enlarged view.) Almost done! Fold and unfold.

(12) Fold one flap down.

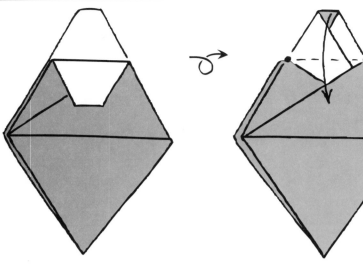
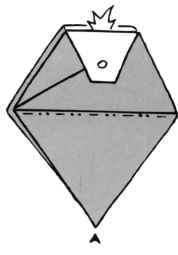

(13) Turn over.

(14) Fold the other flap down too.

(15) Now pull the two flaps. The bottom will flatten out and . . .

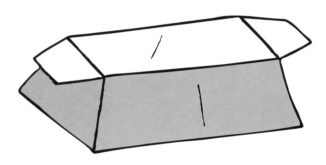

(16) . . . you're done!

About the Creator

Natalia's introduction to origami was in a kindergarten more than twenty years ago. Her nurse showed her how to fold a hen from a square, and it was a real miracle for Natalia! Unfortunately at that time there were no Russian origami books, and thus her further acquaintance with paperfolding was postponed for a long time. Then in *Family and School* magazine she found a set of articles written by Victor Beskrownych, who was the first Russian to begin writing about origami in the former Soviet Union. Now Natalia is the creator of more than twenty origami models. When she wants to create something complex she says that she begins not by folding, but by sculpting the paper!

Natalia Romashova

Goose Balloon
by Dasha Afonkina

In the origami literature there are many variations of the traditional Japanese Crane. This version requires a puff of air to blow it up at the end!

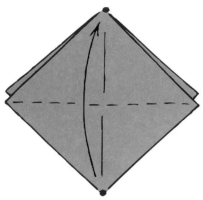

(1) Begin with a Preliminary Fold (see page 121) and position it so that the open end is pointing down. Fold the near layer to the top.

(2) Unfold step 1.

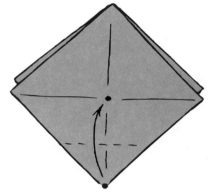

(3) Now fold the bottom corner to the center of the crease you just made.

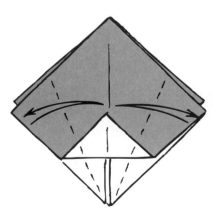

(4) Fold and unfold the lower sides to the center. (Front layers only.)

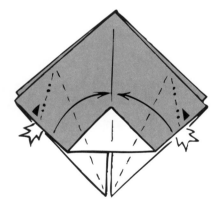

(5) Now, using the creases that you just made, **squash** the side pockets symmetrically. See the next picture, and watch the black triangles.

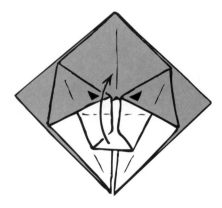

(6) Good! Fold the white flap up.

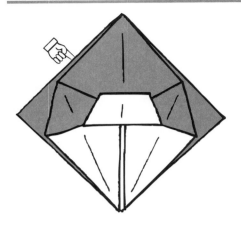

(7) Repeat steps 1-6 on the flipside.

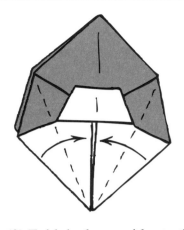

(8) Fold the lower sides to the center.

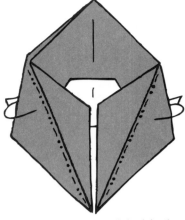

(9) Repeat step 8 behind.

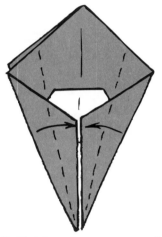

(10) Fold to the center again.

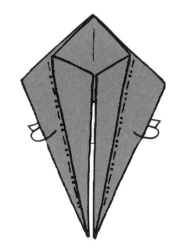

(11) Repeat behind.

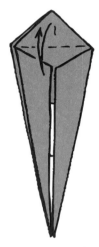

(12) Now the model is nice and skinny. Fold and unfold the top corner down.

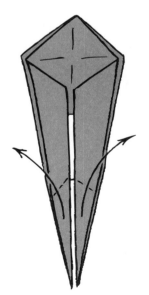

(13) Valley fold the two points up.

(14) This will be the angle of the head and tail. Unfold.

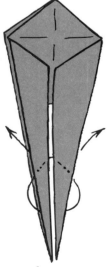

(15) Now use these same creases to reverse-fold the two flaps.

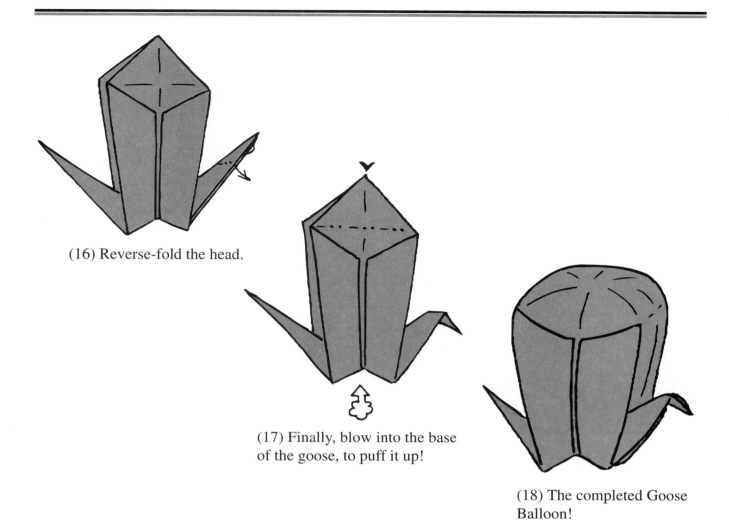

(16) Reverse-fold the head.

(17) Finally, blow into the base of the goose, to puff it up!

(18) The completed Goose Balloon!

About the Creator

It's hard to say what Dasha likes more, to fold or to dance. There are some common features between these two arts, are there not? The esteemed American origami sculptor Michael LaFosse describes paper folding as "dancing with paper." In any case, after studying origami for years, Dasha has decided to dance professionally, and now attends the Acadamy of Russian Ballet. Occasionally she creates some new models, but there is less and less time for such activities. Nevertheless, her parents hope that in the future she might perform a "folded paper dance"!

Dasha Afonkina

Garland

by Sergei Afonkin

This modular ribbon can be used to decorate a tree, a house, or a young person's head. (Young at heart, of course!)

The Unit

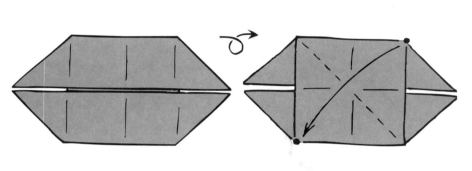

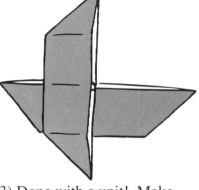

(1) Start with the Pinwheel Base (see page 123). Turn over.

(2) Then fold in half along a diagonal.

(3) Done with a unit! Make several, depending on the size of your garland. (You might need 20 to fit a person's head.)

Locking the Units Together

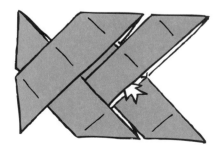

(1) Imagine that the units are fish. Make one fish eat another.

(2) Open up the side of the eaten fish . . .

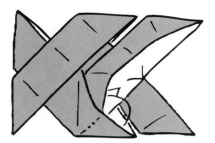 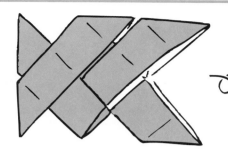 

(3) . . . like this. Tuck the lower jaw of the hungry fish into this pocket, and flatten the model.

(4) Good! Now turn over from left to right.

(5) Open the the eaten fish's pocket on this side. . .

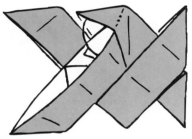 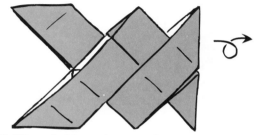

(6) . . . and tuck the upper jaw of the hungry fish inside.

(7) There! Now the two fish are locked, forming a bigger fish! Turn over again.

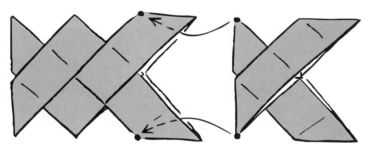

(8) Now have the big fish eat another fish (i.e., unit). Lock them together in the same way.

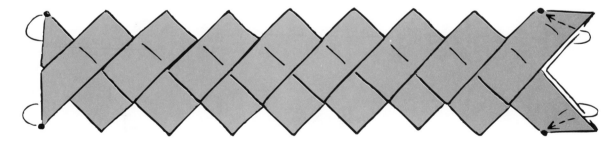

(9) When you have a long enough strip, wrap it around and lock the two ends together. That is, when the fish gets too big and has no other fish to eat, it is forced to eat its own tail! The result is the completed Garland. (It's even a little scaly, like a fish!)

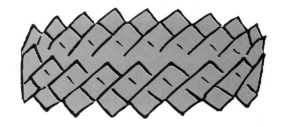

Rocket
by Dima Spiridonov

This wonderful rocket is made three-dimensional by blowing into it at the very end!

(1) Start with a Waterbomb Base. (See page 122.) Fold and unfold one of the flaps to the top corner.

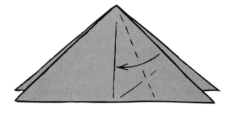

(2) Fold the side edge to the center line.

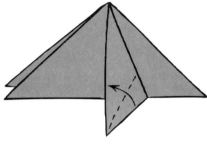

(3) Narrow this point by folding the bottom side to the center line.

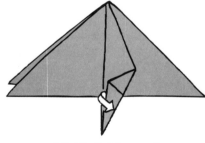

(4) Unfold step 3.

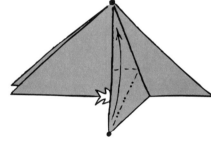

(5) Lift the point all the way to the top. Turn the crease formed in step 3 into a mountain fold as you flatten the model.

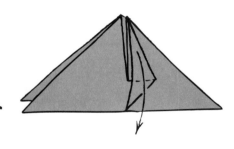

(6) Good! Fold the point back down.

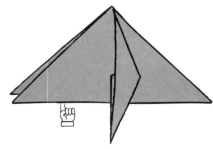

(7) Now repeat steps 1-6 on the left flap.

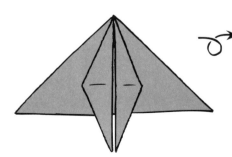

(8) OK! Turn over.

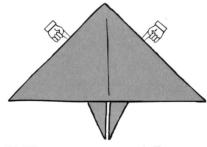

(9) Then repeat steps 1-7 on this side! Wheee!

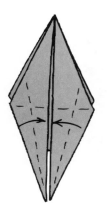 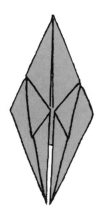 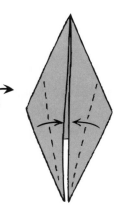 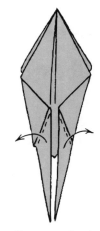

(10) Fold only the near right and left edges to the center.

(11) Turn over.

(12) Do step 10 again.

(13) The flaps at the bottom should be pretty skinny. Fold the near ones to the left and right.

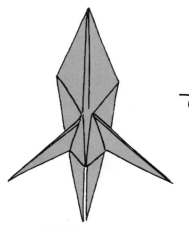 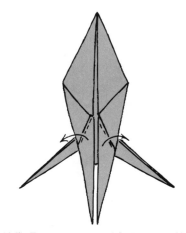 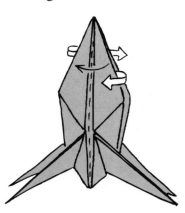

(14) Turn over.

(15) Repeat step 13. Now all the "feet" of the rocket should be in place.

(16) Fold one edge to the left in front and one to the right in back.

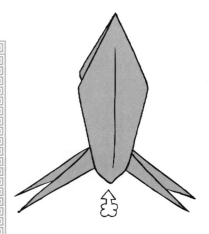 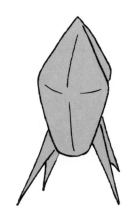

(17) Lastly, blow sharply into the rocket's tailpipe. The model will become 3-D!

(18) The completed Rocket, ready for launching!

Inflatable Rabbit

by Elena Besrukyh

The next two models, both by Elena, make wonderful use of the "blow-up" technique, where air is blown into the model at the end to make it three-dimensional and more life-like.

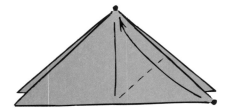

(1) Begin with a Waterbomb Base (see page 122). Fold the lower right corner to the top.

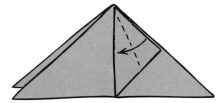

(2) Fold the top edge of this flap to the center line.

(3) Unfold step 2.

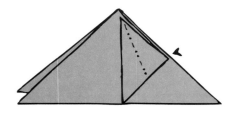

(4) All right! Now use the creases made in step 2 to reverse-fold this corner. All you're really doing is narrowing the point. (Look at the next picture...)

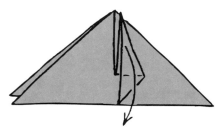

(5) OK! Fold the now-skinny point down. (This will be one of the rabbit's ears.)

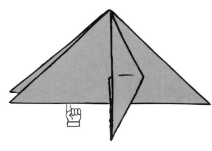

(6) Repeat steps 1-5 on the left.

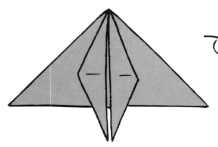

(7) Cool! Turn over.

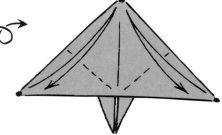

(8) Fold and unfold both flaps to the top.

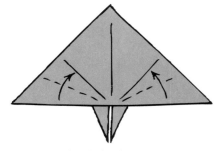

(9) Now fold the bottom edges of these flaps to the crease lines you just made . . .

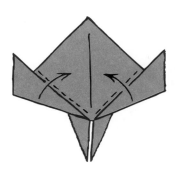

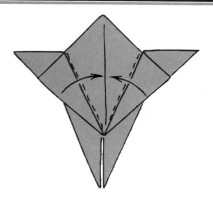

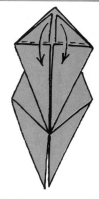

(10) . . . like this. Refold the creases from step 8.

(11) Fold the left and right flaps to the center line.

(12) Fold the two small flaps down. These are the feet!

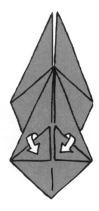

(13) Rotate 180°.

(14) Pull the feet down a little.

(15) Now hold the rabbit's feet with one hand, and the ears with the other. Blow sharply into the rabbit's nose to make it 3-D.

(16) Curl the ears.

Elena Bersrukyh

About the Creator

Russia is a big country, and we have never met Elena personally because she lives in Eastern Russia near Lake Baikal. In her childhood Elena was very involved with painting. After teaching painting in school she began to give lessons in a "young technician's station," a kind of club for kids who like to create things. There Elena became a professional teacher. Her Ph.D. was devoted to origami! Now she is the creator of a set of nice inflatable toys made from the Waterbomb Base.

(17) The finished Rabbit! Draw eyes and whiskers, if you like.

Inflatable Mouse

by Elena Besrukyh

Another creative use of the Waterbomb Base and the "blow-up" technique, this model makes the origami enthusiast wonder, "Why didn't I think of that?"

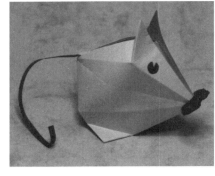

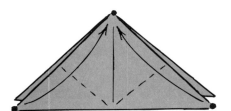

(1) Begin with a Waterbomb Base (see page 122). Fold the front left and right corners to the top.

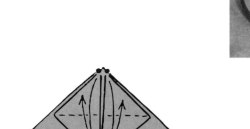

(2) Then fold these flaps down to the bottom center, and back up again.

(3) Fold the lower sides of these flaps to the center line.

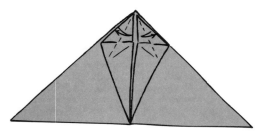

(4) Fold and unfold the top sides of these flaps to the center line.

(5) Now use the existing creases to refold step 4, but this time use the extra paper to pinch a pair of shorter flaps, which will become the mouse's ears!

Джери!

("Jerry!")

Том!

("Tom!")

(6) See the ears? Turn over.

(7) Fold and unfold the two corners to the top.

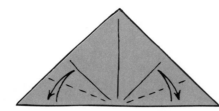

(8) Fold the bottom edges to the crease lines you just made, and unfold.

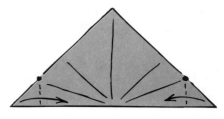

(9) Valley fold the corners, using the previous creases as landmarks.

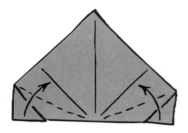

(10) Refold step 8.

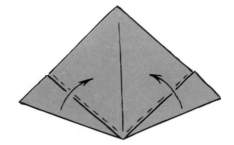

(11) Refold step 7.

(12) Fold the sides to the center line.

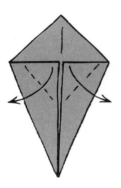

(13) Fold the flaps out to the sides. This will form the little mouse feet!

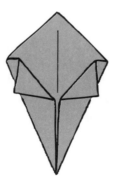

(14) Turn over.

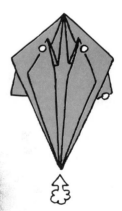

(15) Now comes the blow-up part! Hold the mouse's ears with one hand, and one of the feet with the other while you blow.

(16) The completed Mouse! (You might need to shape the body after blowing it up.) One may draw eyes or tape on a tail for added realism!

Dove Greeting Card
by Elena Afonkina

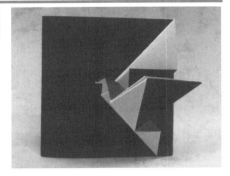

This model is a shining example of "practical origami." From a 1x3 rectangle comes this lovely card, a touching gift for all occasions.

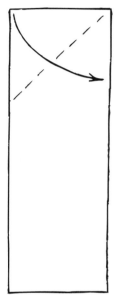

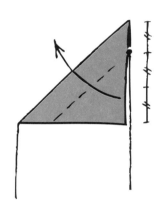

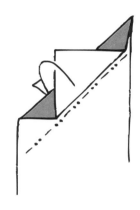

(1) Begin with a 1x3 rectangle. Starting with the white side up will give a colored exterior to the card. Fold the upper left corner down.

(2) Fold the corner back up, making the crease a third of the way down the side.

(3) Mountain-fold behind.

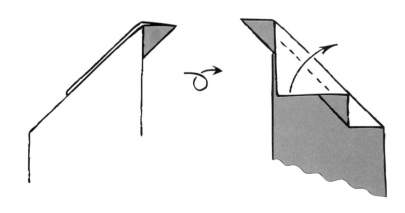

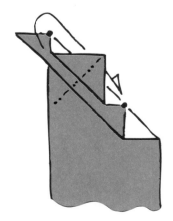

(4) See how the edges are lined up? Turn over.

(5) Fold a single layer up to the right, so that it peeks over the edge. The amount of peekage will determine how big the head is!

(6) Mountain-fold behind along the diagonal of the flap.

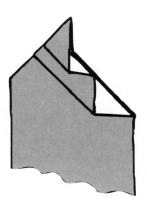

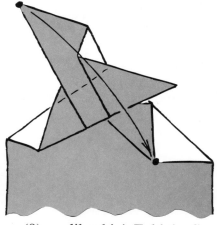

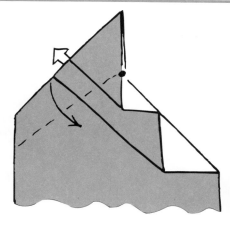

(7) The model should look like this, although since a number of the steps are "judgment folds," your model might look slightly different. Zoom in on the top.

(8) Now fold all the paper over, letting the flaps in the back come up . . .

(9) . . . like this! Fold the flap down to meet the indicated point.

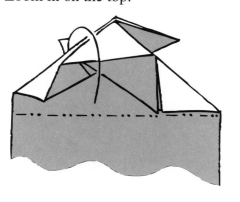

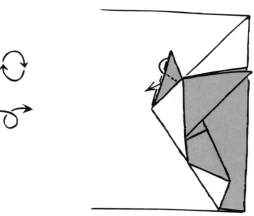

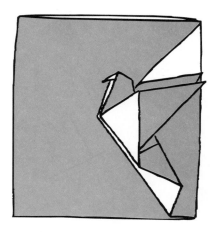

(10) Does it look like a dove yet? No? Well, fold everything behind, rotate the model and turn over.

(11) Make a small reverse fold for the dove's head.

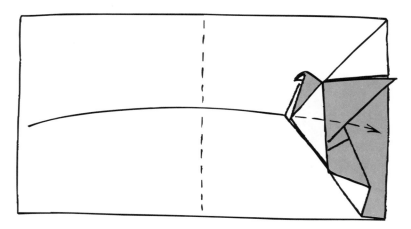

(12) Fold the rest of the rectangle behind the dove. (After writing a suitably romantic message, of course!)

(13) The completed Dove Greeting Card!

Turkmenian Hat
by Yuri Alexandrov

This Turkish Hat, by a Russian paperfolder, can actually be worn if made from large enough paper—say, a 1 foot square.

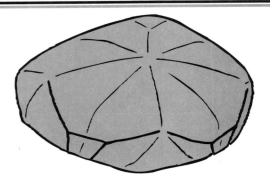

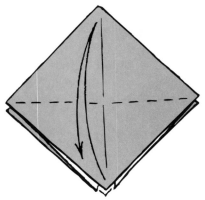

(1) Begin with a Preliminary Fold. (See page 121.) Fold and unfold one layer.

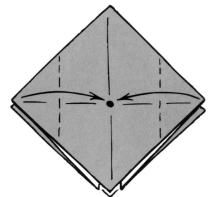

(2) Fold the two front side corners to the center.

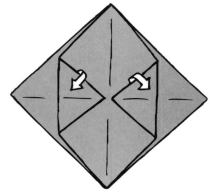

(3) Unfold step 2.

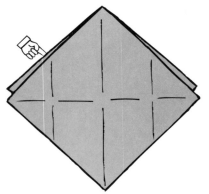

(4) Repeat steps 1-3 behind.

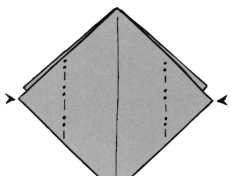

(5) Reverse-fold the left and right corners inside. Use the creases from step 2!

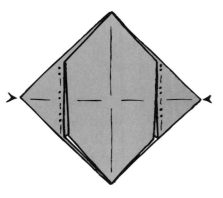

(6) Repeat step 5 with the remaining outer corners.

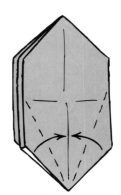

(7) Fold one layer to the center line, left and right.

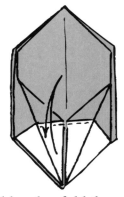

(8) Fold and unfold the white point.

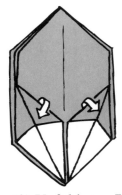

(9) Unfold step 7.

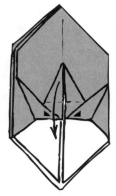

(10) Hey! Now use the existing crease (made in step 8) to fold one layer up.

(11) Narrow the white flap, bringing its outer corners together at the center; watch the black triangles.

(12) Fold the point down.

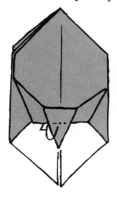

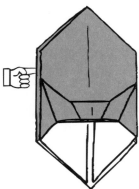

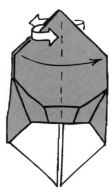

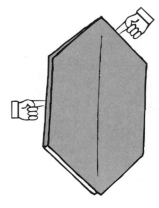

(13) Fold the tip of the flap into the split pocket behind. This will lock it in place.

(14) Repeat steps 7-13 behind.

(15) Fold one section to the right in front, and one to the left behind.

(16) Repeat steps 7-13 in front and back.

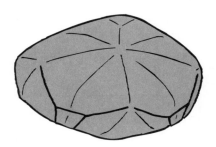

(17) Fold and unfold.

(18) Finally, place your fingers inside the model and spread open the hat.

(19) The completed Turkmenian Hat!

About the Creator

In spite of his youth Yuri is already the creator of ten elegant and original models. He was inspired to create them in his school, where origami has been a regular part of the curriculum for two years, with one lesson a week. The teachers have discovered that after one year of practicing origami, many will try to create original models, as Yuri has done.

Two Cubes
by Elena Afonkina

These two modular cubes take 12 pieces of paper each, and are excellent examples of three-dimensional modular origami, a very popular branch of paperfolding. The first cube is simple in design, while the second (shown to the left) is more ornamental and, thus, more challenging. American Robert Neale was the first to devise this type of modular cube, and many variations have followed.

Cube 1

Twelve squares of paper are needed. Use smallish squares; 3-6 inches each is recommended.

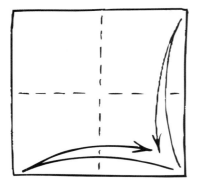

(1) Begin with a square, white side up. Fold and unfold from side to side, in both directions.

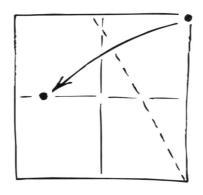

(2) Fold the upper right corner to the horizontal crease, **making sure** that the resulting crease goes through the lower right corner! (Kinda tricky.)

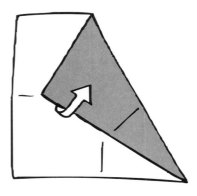

(3) See? Unfold step 2.

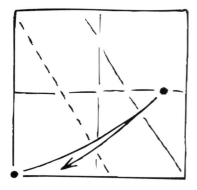

(4) Repeat steps 2-3 with the lower left corner. The crease should be parallel to the one made in step 2.

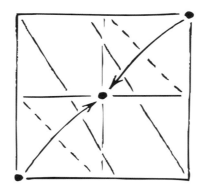

(5) Hoopla! Now fold the upper right and lower left corners to the center.

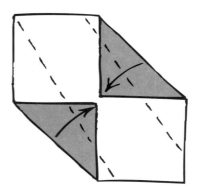

(6) Then refold the creases from steps 2 and 4!

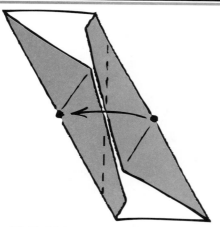  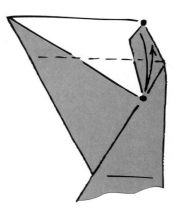

(7) Fold in half, bringing the two points together.

(8) Neat, eh? Zoom in on the top end.

(9) Fold and unfold.

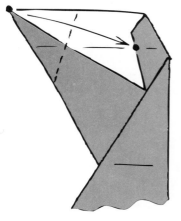 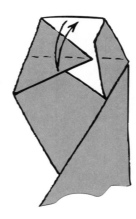 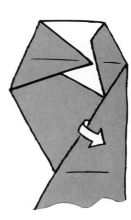

(10) Fold the left corner to the indicated point.

(11) Fold and unfold again. (You need this crease.)

(12) Unfold step 7.

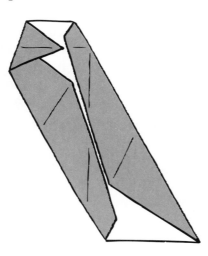 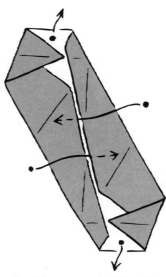

(13) OK! Repeat steps 7-12 on the other end.

(14) Finished with one unit! You'll need a total of 12 of these. The arrows indicate the flaps and pockets of the unit. **Note** that each unit must have the same orientation. If you accidentally fold a "mirror image" of this, then it won't be able to fit into the other ones!

How to Lock the Cube 1 Units Together

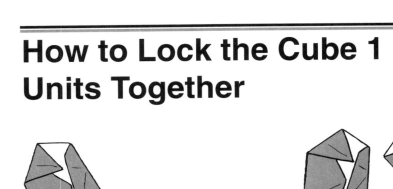

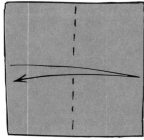

(1) Take two units, and slide the end of one into the inside pocket of the other. The creases should line up.

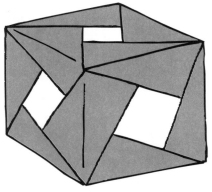

(2) Then slide in a third unit in the same way . . .

(3) . . . the goal being that it takes three units to make a corner of the cube. The ends of the three units will all lock together. Use the crease from step 7 to make the corner become 3-D . . .

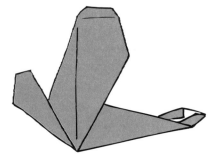

(5) The completed Cube 1! Now get ready for Cube 2!

(4) . . . like this! See how this corner uses exactly one-half of each unit? The other halves will become other corners. Keep adding units, making more corners, until it wraps around and becomes a cube!

Cube 2

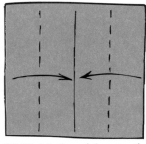

(1) Colored side up. Fold and unfold.

(2) Fold the sides to the center.

(3) Turn over.

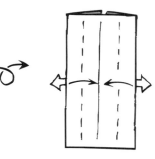

(4) Fold the sides to the center, letting the flaps behind come out.

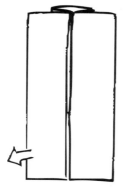 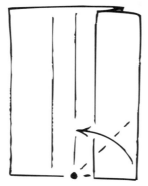  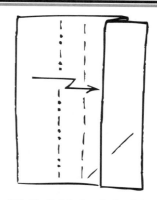

(5) Unfold the left side.

(6) Fold up the lower right corner, making sure to note the landmarks.

(7) Unfold step 6.

(8) Refold the left side.

 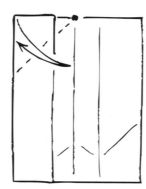  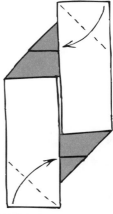

(9) Now unfold the right side.

(10) Fold and unfold the upper left corner and refold the right side.

(11) Now refold the creases from steps 6 and 10, tucking the flaps inside.

(12) Fold the corners toward the center. (The little tips too!)

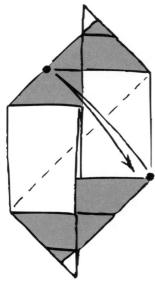 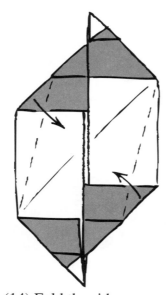  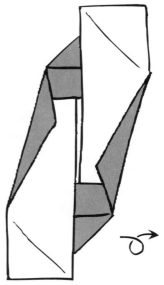

(13) (Enlarged view.) Fold and unfold, noting the landmarks!

(14) Fold the side corners inward as shown.

(15) Unfold step 12.

(16) Turn over, and you've finished one unit! Make eleven more.

How to Put the Cube 2 Units Together

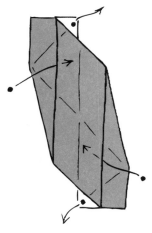

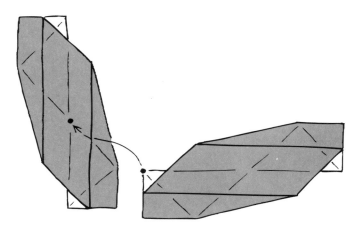

(1) Here we see where the pockets and flaps are in this unit.

(2) Slide a flap of one unit into the pocket of another. Let the dots in the picture guide you in doing this.

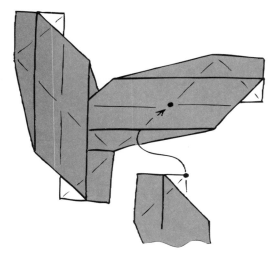

(3) Now add a third unit . . .

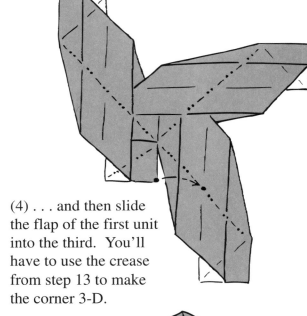

(4) . . . and then slide the flap of the first unit into the third. You'll have to use the crease from step 13 to make the corner 3-D.

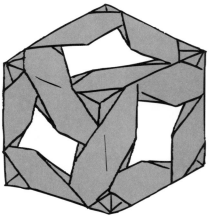

(5) That's one corner! Add units to the other flaps to make more corners, until you get a cube!

(6) The completed Cube 2!

Cat with White Stockings
by Sergei Afonkin

For some reason, there are very few good cat models in the origami canon, perhaps because the graceful curves of the feline are difficult to capture in rigid, angular paper folds. Yet this model, made from European A4 proportioned paper, is unmistakably catty!

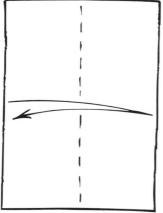

(1) Begin with an A4 rectangle. (See page 52.) Fold and unfold in half lengthwise.

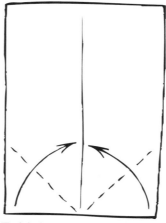

(2) Fold the bottom corners to the center line.

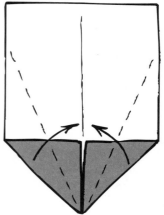

(3) Fold again to the center line, as if you were making an airplane.

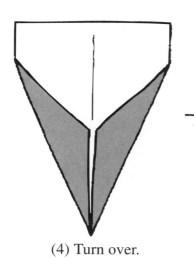

(4) Turn over.

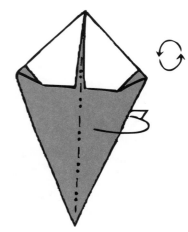

(5) Now fold the top corners to the center line.

(6) Mountain-fold in half, away from you, and rotate.

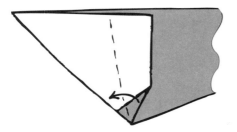

(7) (Enlarged view.) Fold the bottom angle in half.

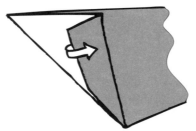

(8) Unfold step 7.

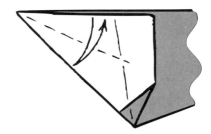

(9) Fold and unfold the top edge of the flap to the folded edge.

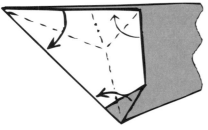

(10) OK. Use the creases from steps 7 and 9 to collapse the flap, pinching a new small point as you do so . . .

(11) . . . like this! Maneuvers like this are known as **rabbit ear** folds in the origami world, but in this case it's a cat's ear! Repeat steps 7-10 behind.

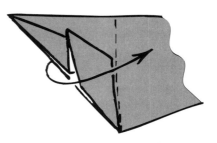

(12) Fold to the right.

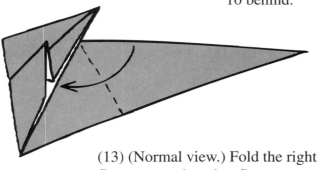

(13) (Normal view.) Fold the right flap to meet the other flap.

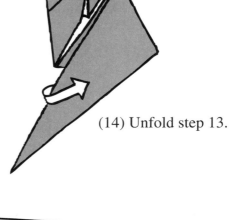

(14) Unfold step 13.

(15) Now open up the left flap and squash it down symmetrically.

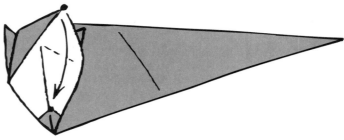

(16) Step 15 in progress . . .

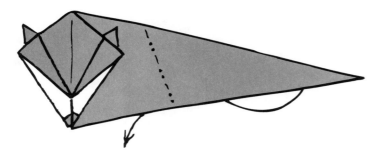

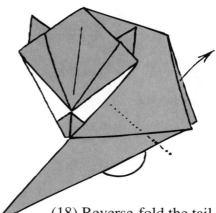

(17) . . . and step 15 is done! See the cat's face? Then use the crease from step 13 to reverse-fold the tail down.

(18) Reverse-fold the tail back up into the groove. This puts the tail in position and creates small rear feet for the kitty.

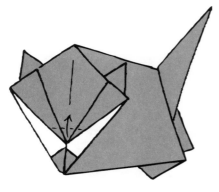

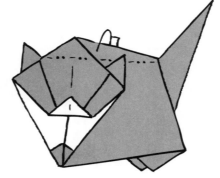

(19) Fold the flap up a little to make a cat nose.

(20) Slim the body with a mountain fold at the top.

(21) Open the bottom a bit, so that the cat can stand, and you're done!

(22) The completed Cat with White Stockings!

Snail Runny
by Irina Smirnova

There aren't many origami snail models. This one is quite a charmer!

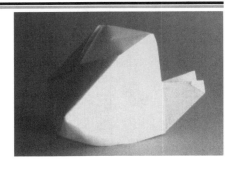

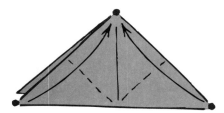

(1) Begin with a Waterbomb Base. (See page 122.) Fold the front lower flaps to the top.

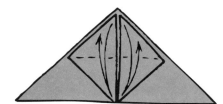

(2) Fold and unfold the flaps to the bottom center.

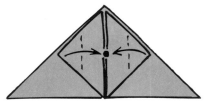

(3) Fold the side corner of each flap to the center.

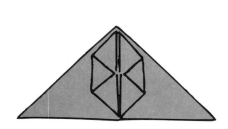

(4) Zoom in on the center part.

(5) Fold the two top flaps to the center.

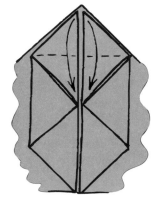

(6) Fold and unfold these flaps right along the line where the folded edges meet.

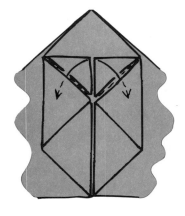

(7) Now refold the creases you make in the previous step, but this time tuck the flaps into the pockets.

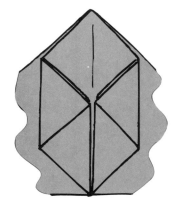

(8) OK! Zoom back out.

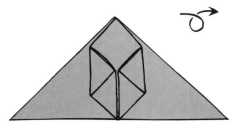

(9) Turn over.

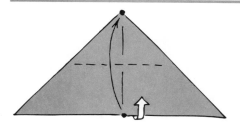

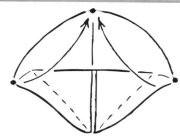

(10) Bring the center of the bottom edge to the top point. The model will become 3-D. . .

(11) Then flatten everything by bringing the corners of the paper to the top center point as well . . .

(12) . . . like this! Fold the corners to the sides.

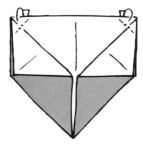

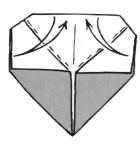

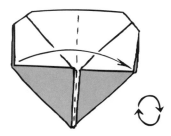

(13) Mountain-fold little corners behind.

(14) Make valley creases on the near layer. (These will be used later.)

(15) Fold in half. Rotate as shown.

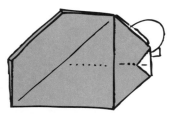

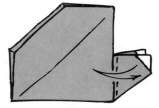

(16) Lift the near left flap up. Repeat behind.

(17) Now there is a layer of paper inside that you want to reverse-fold down. This uses the creases made in step 14.

(18) Fold and unfold. Repeat behind.

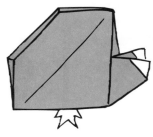

(19) Now open up the snail's shell by putting your fingers in the bottom opening.

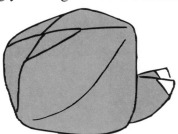

(20) The completed Snail!

About the Creator

Irina lives in Moscow. She is a student at the Moscow Teacher Training University, Department of Art and Design. In addition she runs an origami children's group in a Kuntsevo district. Origami experts know that it's not easy to create good, new models from the heavily-used Waterbomb Base, but Irina has done just this! Her snail captures what many origami masters strive for—simplicity and expressiveness at the same time. Irina has a good sense of humor and knowledge of English. It was she who named her model "Snail Runny"!

Elephant
by Eugeni Fridryh

There are many elephants in the origami kingdom, and this design by Eugeni is a wonderful addition.

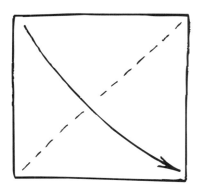

(1) Begin with the square white side up. Fold a diagonal.

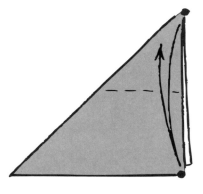

(2) Fold and unfold the top point to the bottom.

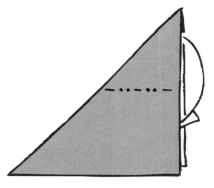

(3) Use the crease from step 2 to reverse-fold the point inside.

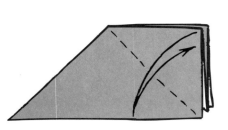

(4) Fold and unfold one flap down.

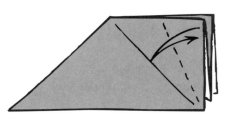

(5) Fold and unfold the side of the flap to the crease line.

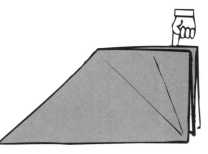

(6) Repeat steps 4-5 behind.

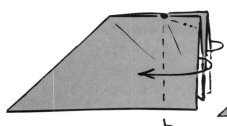

(7) OK. At the spot where the crease from step 5 hits the top edge, pull the paper to the left in front and in back. At the same time, form the trunk . . .

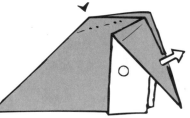

(8) . . . like this! Hold the model at the indicated spot and raise the trunk. This will cause the paper to slide along the back. That's OK. Flatten the model.

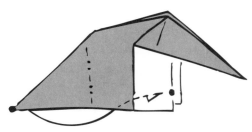

(9) Great! Reverse-fold the tail inside the elephant.

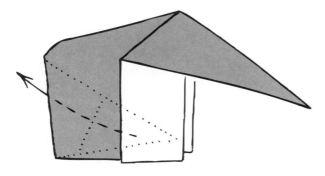

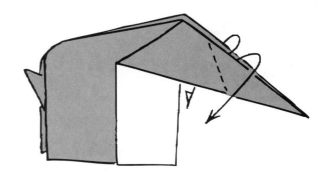

(10) Reverse-fold the tail back out, making sure that it protrudes enough to create the illusion of an elephant's tail.

(11) Now turn the trunk inside-out (this is called an **outside reverse fold**!) to put the trunk into position.

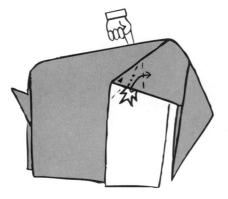

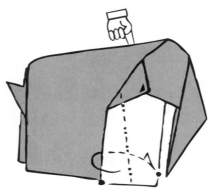

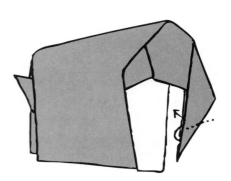

(12) Pull the nearest layer to the right and flatten to make an ear; watch the black triangle. **Repeat behind**.

(13) Mountain-fold inside.

(14) Make a little reverse fold for the tip of the trunk.

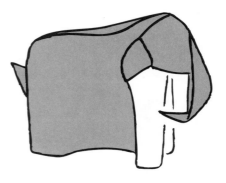

(15) Carefully shape the elephant by rounding the top and making mountain folds on the bottom. The model will become 3-D.

(16) The completed Elephant!

Rabbit

by Alexander Tupin

This little rabbit is cute and friendly, although its folding sequence has a few tricky maneuvers.

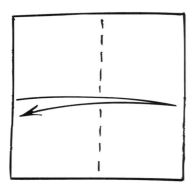

(1) Begin with the square white side up. Fold and unfold.

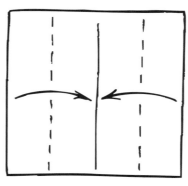

(2) Fold the two sides to the center line.

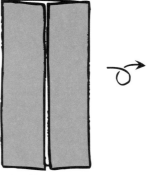

(3) Turn over.

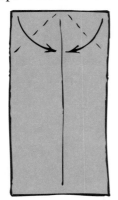

(4) Fold the top corners to the center.

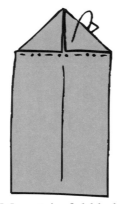

(5) Mountain-fold behind.

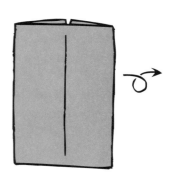

(6) Wicked! Turn over again.

(7) Unfold step 4.

(8) Unfold step 5!

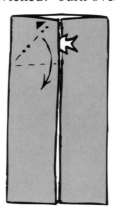

(9) Now use the creases to pull down the corner into a triangle.

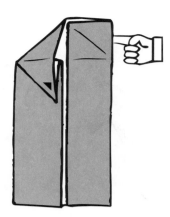 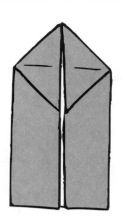 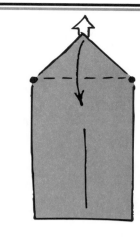

(10) Repeat step 9 on the right.

(11) Turn ova.

(12) Fold the top point down, letting the flaps behind come up.

 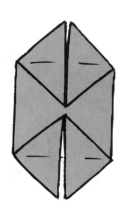 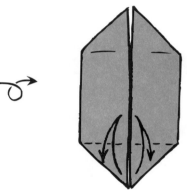

(13) Repeat steps 4-12 on the bottom.

(14) Turn over.

(15) Fold and unfold the two bottom flaps.

 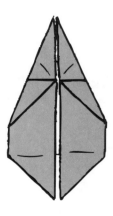 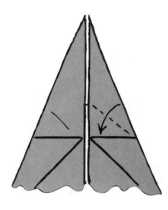

(16) Fold the top edges to the center line.

(17) Cool! Zoom in on the top.

(18) Fold the right flap down to a horizontal position . . .

(19) Unfold step 18.

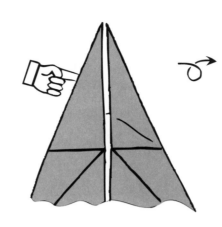

(20) Repeat steps 18-19 on the left. Turn over.

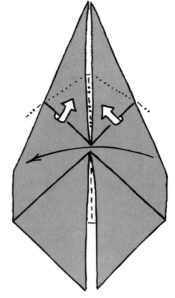

(21) (Normal view.) Fold leftward in half, but let the ears and head pivot up clockwise. . .

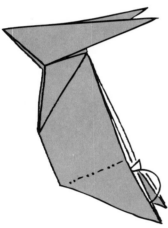

(22) . . . like this. Reverse-fold one of the bottom flaps inside.

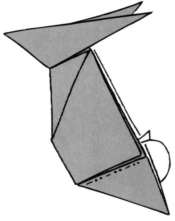

(23) Repeat step 22 with the other flap.

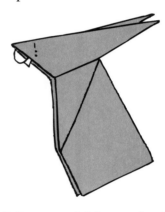

(24) Reverse-fold to make the nose.

(25) OK. Now create an ear by opening one of the flaps and flattening it upward.

(26) Repeat for the other ear.

(27) X-ray view! Fold one of the inside flaps over so that it sticks out.

(28) See? This will become the tail. Reverse-fold to make the tail round.

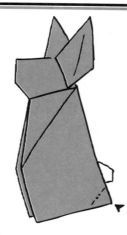

(29) Make another reverse fold to round out the body.

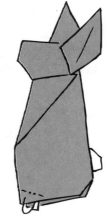

(30) Mountain-fold one flap inside.

(31) Then fold the back flap inside as well. This finishes rounding off the body.

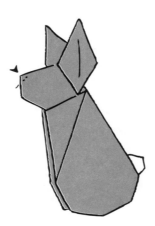

(32) One more tiny reverse fold will smooth out the nose.

(33) The completed Bunny!

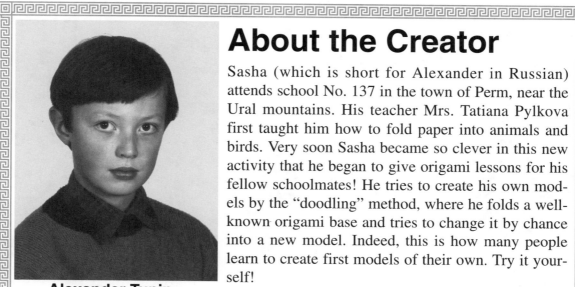

About the Creator

Sasha (which is short for Alexander in Russian) attends school No. 137 in the town of Perm, near the Ural mountains. His teacher Mrs. Tatiana Pylkova first taught him how to fold paper into animals and birds. Very soon Sasha became so clever in this new activity that he began to give origami lessons for his fellow schoolmates! He tries to create his own models by the "doodling" method, where he folds a well-known origami base and tries to change it by chance into a new model. Indeed, this is how many people learn to create first models of their own. Try it yourself!

Alexander Tupin

Baby Dragon
by Liana Andreeva

This fun Baby Dragon is an action model—it can flap its wings! The folding sequence for this model is long, making it a challenge. Be sure to take care in the precise location of the folds.

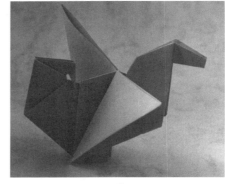

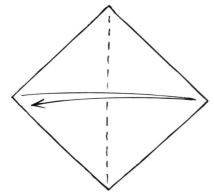

(1) White side up. Fold and unfold a diagonal.

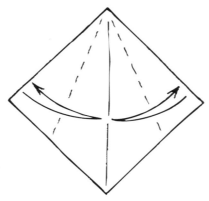

(2) Fold and unfold the top edges to the center line.

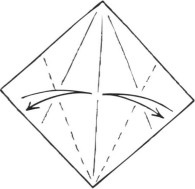

(3) Repeat step 2 with the bottom sides.

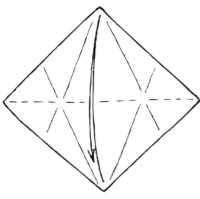

(4) Fold and unfold the other diagonal.

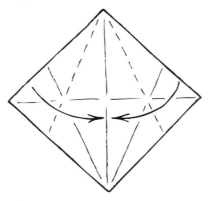

(5) Now refold the creases from step 2.

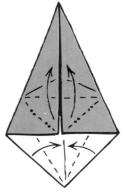

(6) Refold the lower edges to the center line, but allow the internal corners to form points . . .

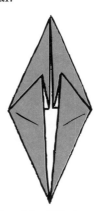

(7) . . . like this. We have folded the Fish Base, which can also make dragons.

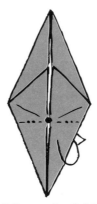

(8) Mountain-fold the bottom point behind.

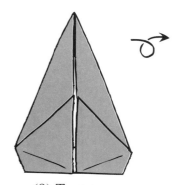

(9) Turn over.

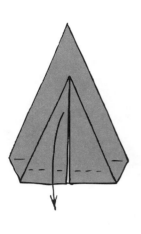 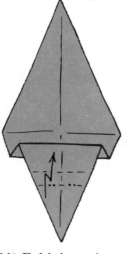 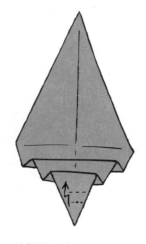 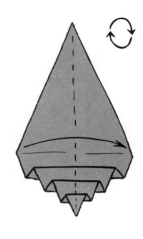

(10) Fold the point down.

(11) Fold the point up and down again to make another pleat.

(12) Do it one more time.

(13) Then fold in half. Rotate the model.

(14) Now pivot the small flap clockwise and flatten the model. This will make tiny creases inside the dragon.

(15) In this way we will form the tail! Pivot the next section of the tail up and flatten.

(16) See? Do it one more time.

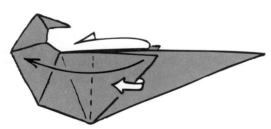

(17) Fold the side flaps to the left, in front and in back.

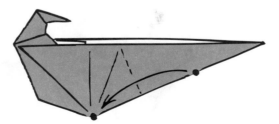

(18) Fold the right flap down to the left, making sure the crease is positioned as shown!

(19) Crease firmly, and unfold step 18.

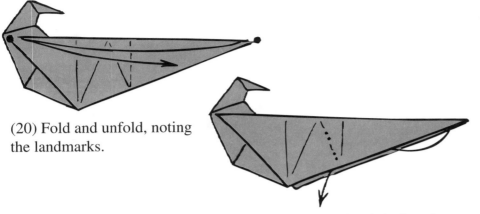

(20) Fold and unfold, noting the landmarks.

(21) Reverse-fold the right flap down, using the crease from step 18.

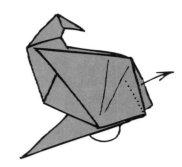

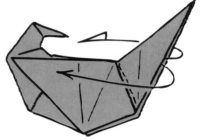

(22) Reverse-fold the point back up, this time using the crease from step 20 . . .

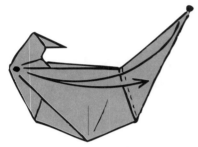

(23) . . . like this. Fold and unfold along the folded edge.

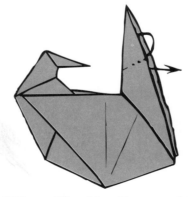

(24) Fold and unfold the right side of the flap to the folded edge.

(25) Reverse-fold the flap inside-out using the crease from step 23 . . .

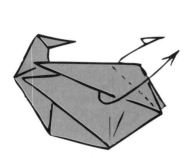

(26) . . . like this. Turn the flap inside-out again, this time using the crease from step 24 . . .

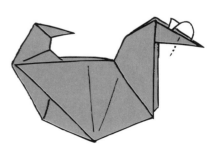

(27) . . . like this. Reverse-fold the head . . .

(28) . . . and square the head off with another tiny reverse fold.

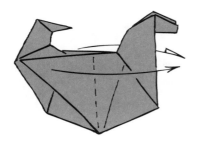

(29) Fold the wings forward.

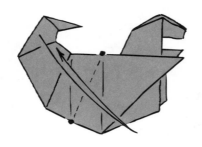

(30) Fold and unfold through **all layers**, noting the landmarks!

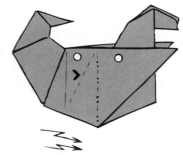

(31) Hold as shown and swing the whole body counterclockwise between the wings; front and back must be symmetrical.

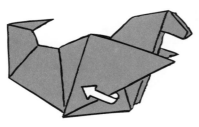

(32) Swing the wings to the left.

(33) Fold the near corner to the crease line, and unfold . . .

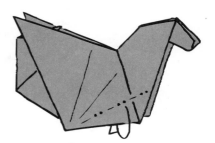

(34) . . . and then use this crease to mountain-fold the corner inside.

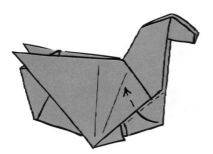

(35) Fold the back corner inside as well.

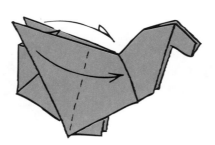

(36) Fold the wings patially rightward, and you're done with the Baby Dragon!

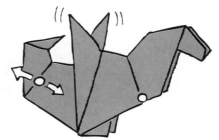

To make the wings flap: Hold at the indicated spots and pull gently.

About the Creator of the Baby Dragon

Liana lives far from the western part of Russia, near the bank of the great Volga River in the town of Cheboksary. Her creative ability in paper folding was inspired by an origami exhibition made by the St. Petersburg Origami Center in November 1993 with the help of Irina Kapitonova, a mathematics teacher in Cheboksary. It was dark in Liana's city, not only in the physical sense (due to its northern latitude) but because the country had been going through a very hard period at that time. Yet the lights of origami touched her heart, and now she wants to be an origami teacher!

Liana Andreeva

Baby Dragons in flight.

Shovel

by Sergei Afonkin

This paper Shovel is folded from a 2x1 rectangle. Make one using stiff paperboard and take it to the beach!

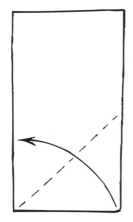

(1) Start with a 2x1 rectangle. Fold a diagonal at the bottom.

(2) Unfold.

(3) Fold the other diagonal and unfold.

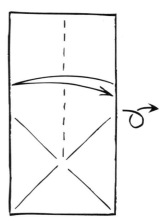

(4) Fold and unfold down the middle, but not all the way down. Turn over.

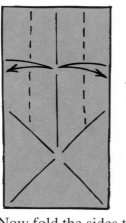

(5) Now fold the sides to the center, but make the creases go down only as far as the diagonal creases. Turn over.

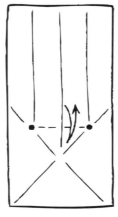

(6) Pinch another crease as shown.

(7) Lastly, pinch diagonal creases as shown.

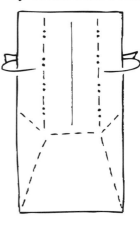

(8) Now form the shovel by wrapping the top edges behind and using the valley folds at the bottom . . .

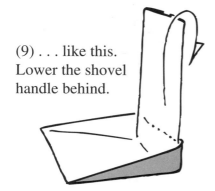

(9) . . . like this. Lower the shovel handle behind.

(10) Roll up a handle . . .

(11) . . . and you're done with the Shovel!

Clapping Clown
by Elena Afonkina

This is another action model—the clown claps its hands for you when you move it!

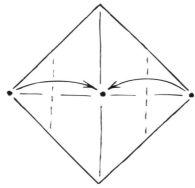

(1) White side up. Fold and unfold both diagonals.

(2) Fold the left and right corners to the center.

(3) Mountain-fold the top corner behind to the center.

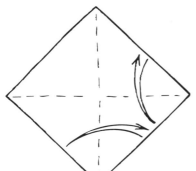

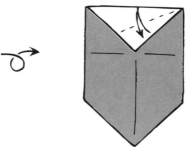

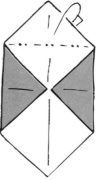

(4) Turn over.

(5) Fold and unfold the side of the white flap to the top edge.

(6) Do the same thing in the other direction.

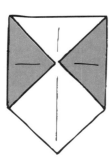

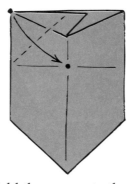

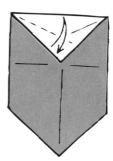

(7) Now use these creases to fold the flap up, pinching a new point in the process, i.e. a rabbit ear.

(8) Fold the corner to the center.

(9) Fold the small flap to the left.

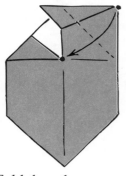

(10) Fold the other corner to the center point.

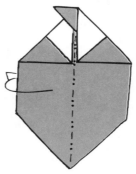

(11) Mountain-fold in half, away from you.

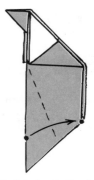

(12) Fold the left side so that it touches the corner.

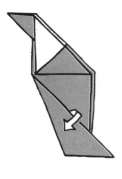

(13) Unfold step 12.

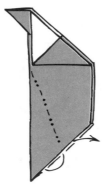

(14) Use this crease to reverse-fold.

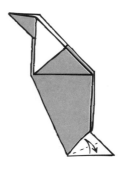

(15) Fold and unfold.

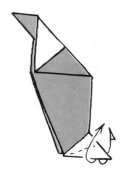

(16) Outside reverse-fold to make the foot.

(17) Now open up the clown and pull out the hidden paper. This will form the arms and make the model 3-D . . .

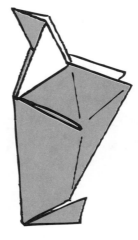

(18) . . . like this. Done with the Clapping Clown!

To make it clap, hold the foot and pull the head back and forth.

Monster of Inflation

by Sergei Afonkin

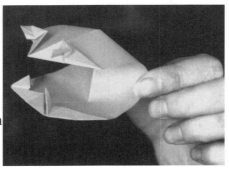

This model—also known as "Prices Bite!"—is made from a dollar bill, and symbolizes the hungry nature of money. In Russia, American dollars are actually quite common, so it is not surprising that a Russian would invent an origami model folded from a dollar bill.

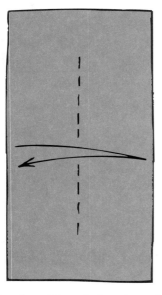

(1) Begin with a dollar (or a 3x7 rectangle). It doesn't matter which side is up. Crease in half, the long way, but it doesn't need to go all the way to the ends. Turn over.

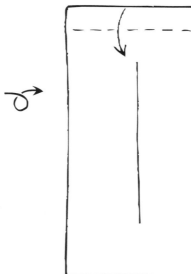

(2) Fold the top edge down a little.

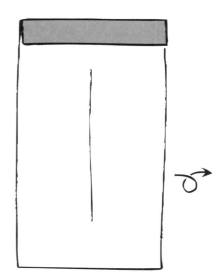

(3) Turn over.

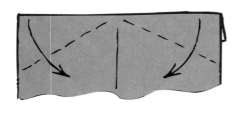

(4) Zoom in on the top end. Fold the left and right corners down at an angle.

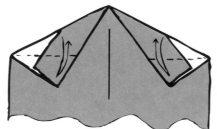

(5) Fold and unfold the flaps back to the top.

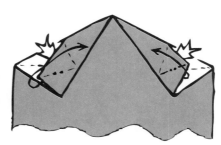

(6) Lift the single-layer corner at the left and swing it upward clockwise; flatten it into a rabbit ear. Repeat at the right.

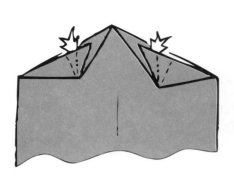

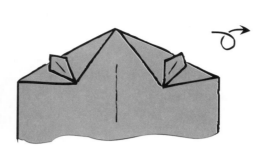

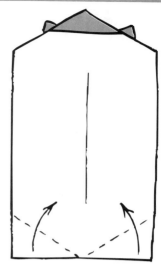

(7) Squash the small flaps evenly. These will become the eyes of the "monster."

(8) You're done with the eyes! Zoom back out and turn over.

(9) Fold the bottom corners up at an angle, and zoom in.

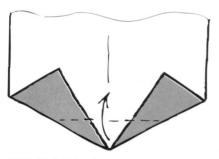

(10) Fold the bottom point up.

(11) Pinch the two side points in half with mountain folds. This will cause some of the paper on the sides to slide over . . .

(12) . . . like this. Lift the two points so that they stand up from the model. These will be the teeth!

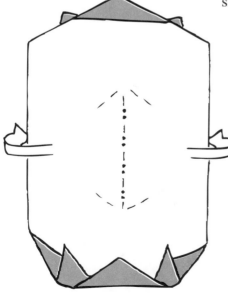

(14) . . . like this! Pinch the sides together with your fingers, and the Monster will bite!

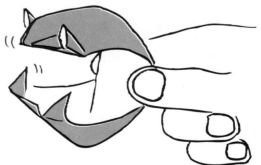

(13) Finally, use the center crease to wrap the sides behind, while letting the top and bottom curl over in front . . .

Warning: Do not scare small children with money.

Goose Box

by Dasha Afonkina

This model, similar to a classic "traditional" box, was independently discovered by young Dasha. The reader may have wondered why both of Dasha's models in this book are named "goose." This is because her nickname at home is "Gosling." Blame your father, Dasha!

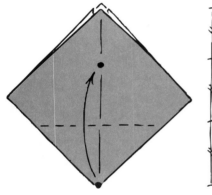

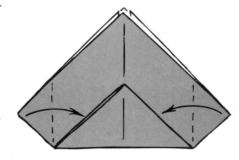

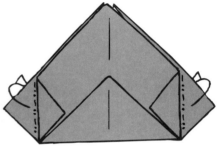

(1) Begin with a Preliminary Fold (see page 121) and position it so that the open end is pointing up. Fold the bottom corner a third of the way up.

(2) Fold the front left and right flaps to the folded edge.

(3) Mountain-fold the back flaps behind by the same amount.

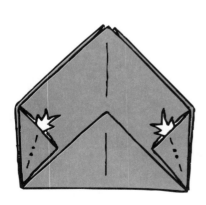

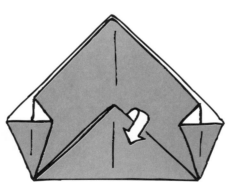

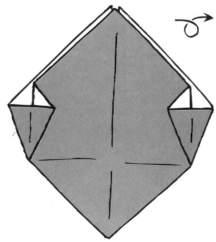

(4) Open up the small left and right flaps and squash them flat symmetrically.

(5) Swing the big flap back down.

(6) Turn over.

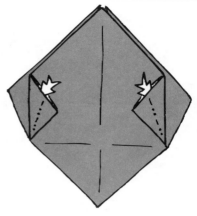

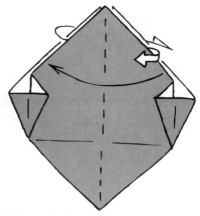

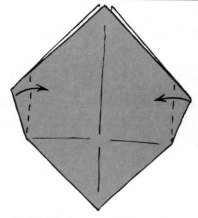

(7) Squash the small flaps so that they line up with the other pair.

(8) Then fold one flap in front to the left and one in back to the right.

(9) Fold the small flaps in.

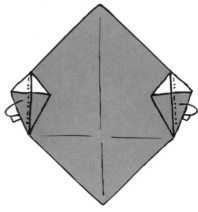

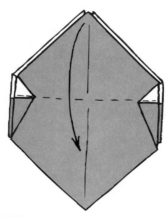

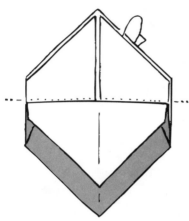

(10) Repeat step 9 behind.

(11) Now fold one layer down as far as possible.

(12) Repeat step 11 behind.

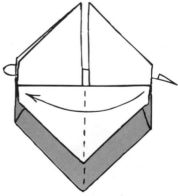

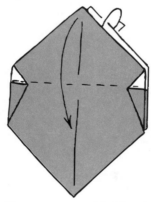

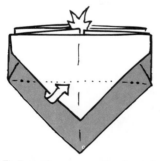

(13) Again, fold one flap to the left and one to the right.

(14) Repeat steps 11-12 with these flaps.

(15) Lastly, open the box by putting your fingers inside and spreading out the bottom.

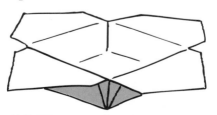

(16) The completed Goose Box!

Box for Sweets

by Marina Putrenko

This elegant box can also be found in some Japanese origami books. Marina created this model on her own, in a country far, far away!

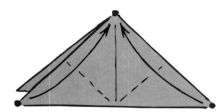

(1) Begin with a Waterbomb Base. (See page 122.) Fold the two front corners to the top.

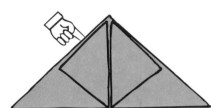

(2) Repeat step 1 behind.

(3) (Enlarged view!) Open up the two flaps in the front and squash them; watch the black triangles.

(4) Repeat step 3 behind.

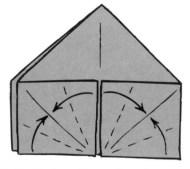

(5) Fold the sides of each square to the diagonal center line . . .

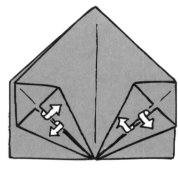

(6) . . . like this. Unfold step 5.

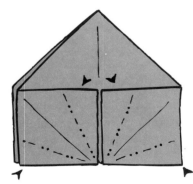

(7) Now use the creases from step 5 to reverse-fold the sides of the squares inside . . .

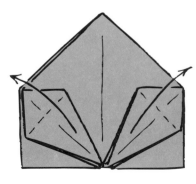

(8) . . . like this. Fold the resulting flaps diagonally upward.

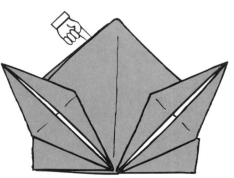

(9) Repeat steps 5-8 behind.

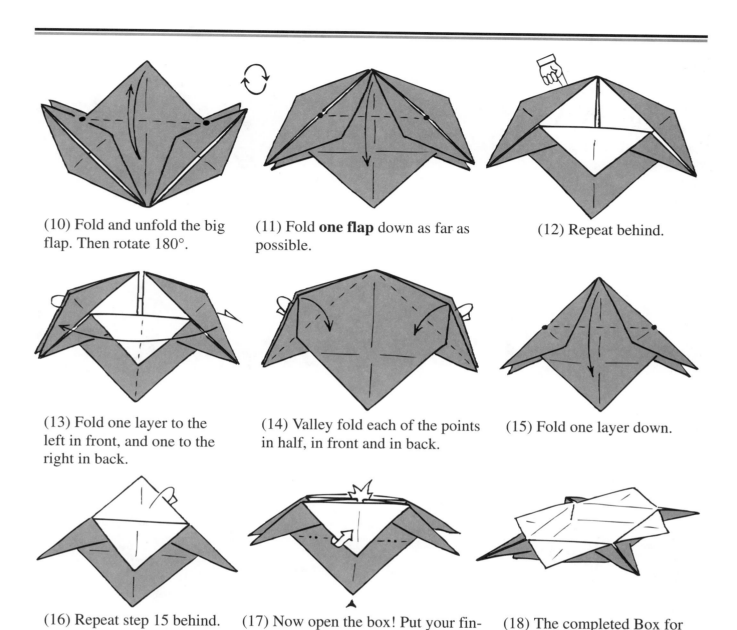

(10) Fold and unfold the big flap. Then rotate 180°.

(11) Fold **one flap** down as far as possible.

(12) Repeat behind.

(13) Fold one layer to the left in front, and one to the right in back.

(14) Valley fold each of the points in half, in front and in back.

(15) Fold one layer down.

(16) Repeat step 15 behind.

(17) Now open the box! Put your fingers inside and flatten the bottom.

(18) The completed Box for Sweets! (Or whatever else you wish to place inside.)

About the Creator

Marina lives in Moscow. Her first original origami invention was an airplane—not the classic paper airplane, but a variation. At that time it was very unusual to think of a paper airplane as someone's invention. For decades Russian children have been folding paper airplanes, just like American children, passing the secret of folding such planes by word-of-mouth from generation to generation. Until 1996 there were no Russian books devoted to paper airplanes made by different creators. Thus it is possible that Marina's airplane was the first "original" Russian paper plane design! She has also created other nice models, one of which you see on this page.

Vase
by Elena Afonkina

This wonderful geometric vase of Elena's was originally titled "Vase—Do Not Take Sweets!" It was independently discovered by Philip Shen of Hong Kong and is very similar to a Vase from the Spanish paperfolding tradition (circa 1939). A hexagonal sheet of paper is needed to fold it.

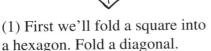
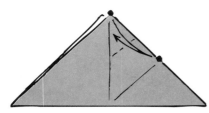

(1) First we'll fold a square into a hexagon. Fold a diagonal.

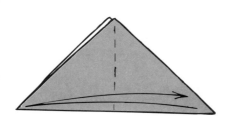

(2) Fold and unfold.

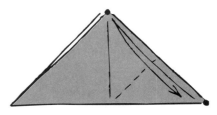

(3) Fold the right corner to the top and unfold.

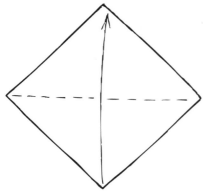

(4) Fold the middle of the right side to the top and unfold, but don't make the crease very long!

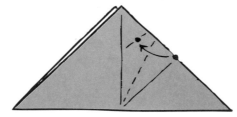

(5) Now fold the middle of the right side to the crease you just made, making sure the crease goes through the bottom center point . . .

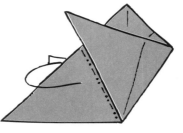

(6) . . . like this! This creates a 60° angle. Fold the left corner behind so that it's flush with the folded edge.

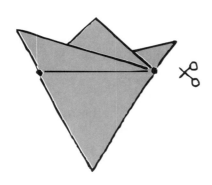

(7) Then cut straight across, from corner to corner.

(8) Open up the result, and you'll have a hexagon!

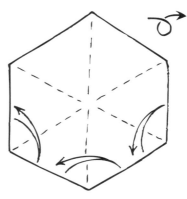

(9) Crease all three diagonals of the hexagon. Turn over.

 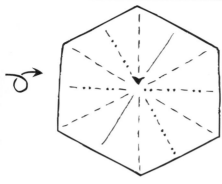 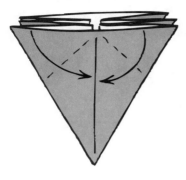

(10) Fold the hexagon from side to side three times. Then turn over again!

(11) Now collapse the hexagon symmetrically . . .

(12) . . . like this. Fold the front two flaps to the center line.

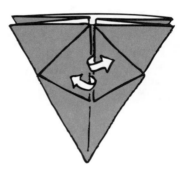 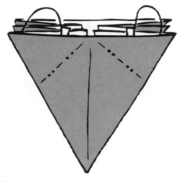 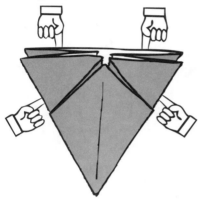

(13) Unfold step 12.

(14) Use these creases to reverse-fold the two corners inside . . .

(15) . . . like this. Repeat on the other 4 flaps.

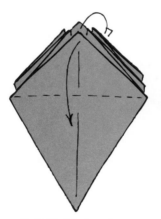 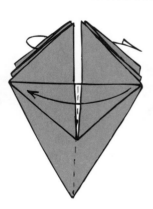 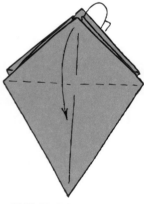 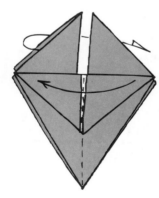

(16) Fold the front and back flaps down.

(17) Fold to the left in front and to the right in back.

(18) Fold the front and back flaps down.

(19) Repeat steps 17-18 on the last pair of flaps.

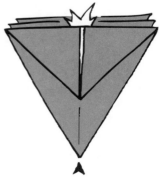

(20) Finally, open up the Vase. You'll need to flatten the bottom and pull the inside corners of the hexagon out, then the Vase is done!

Chinese Table
by Maria Gorbunova

This model closely resembles Philip Shen's Incense Burner. Notice that while this table is challenging to fold (it requires much precreasing at the outset), it is structurally quite simple!

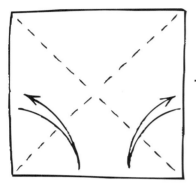

(1) White side up. Fold and unfold both diagonals. Turn over.

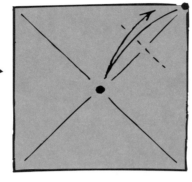

(2) Fold and unfold one corner to the center, **but don't** make the crease go all the way across! Just have it straddle the diagonal line.

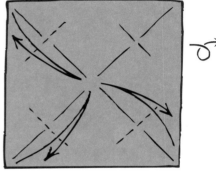

(3) Repeat step 2 on the other three corners. Turn over again.

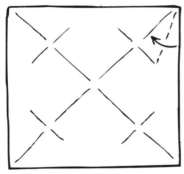

(4) Fold the right edge to the diagonal, but again, don't make it go all the way across!

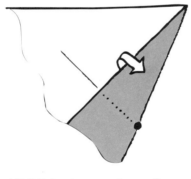

(5) Make it go only as far as this. Unfold.

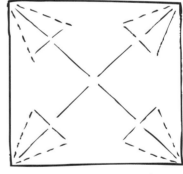

(6) Repeat this 7 more times.

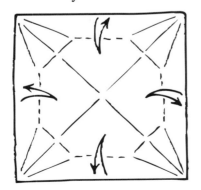

(7) Add four more creases as shown.

(8) Now fold two opposite corners, letting the rest become 3-D . . .

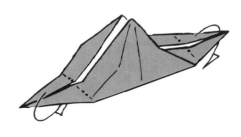

(9) . . . like this! Mountain-fold the two flat corners underneath.

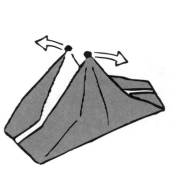

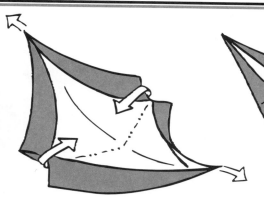

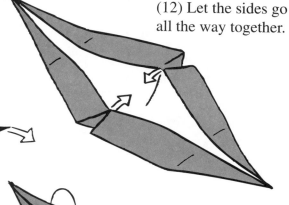

(12) Let the sides go all the way together.

(10) Pull apart the two points . . .

(11) . . . and let the sides come together. Mountain creases should form inside.

(13) Now mountain-fold these two flat flaps underneath.

(14) Open up the center and adjust the legs.

About the Creator

The first origami model created by this young girl was published in a Russian origami textbook for primary schools. This edition was approved by the Russian Ministry of Education and is now being used in many towns. Maria's other origami creation is the Chinese Table, presented here. The model is a masterpiece of elegance. With just a few creases Maria was able to make an unexpected three-dimensional object that is very stable!

Maria Gorbunova

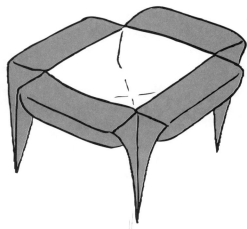

(15) The completed Chinese Table!

Four-Heart Box
by Elena Afonkina

This beautiful box is decorated with hearts! Amazingly enough, it is very much in the style of origami designer Francis Ow of Singapore, although the design is original with Elena.

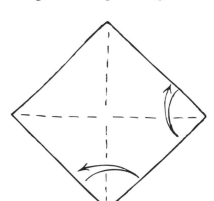

(1) White side up. Fold and unfold both diagonals.

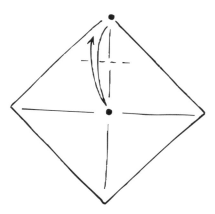

(2) Fold and unfold the top corner to the center, but **only pinch** the crease in the middle!

(3) Fold the top corner to this pinch mark and unfold.

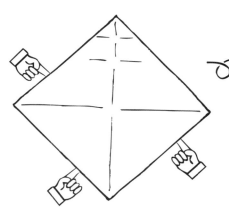

(4) Repeat steps 2-3 on the other corners. Then turn over!

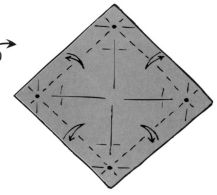

(5) Fold and unfold each side in, making sure to note the landmarks!

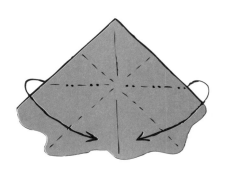

(6) (Enlarged view.) Use the existing creases to collapse a corner . . .

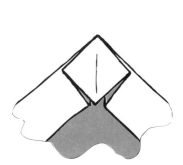

(7) . . . like this. You'll have to do this on all four corners . . .

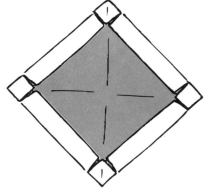

(8) . . . to get this! OK, zoom back in on one of the corners.

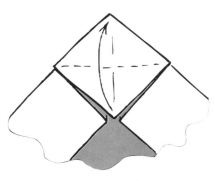

(9) Fold the flap up.

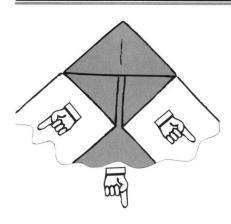

(10) Ta-da! Repeat step 9 on the other corners. Zoom back out.

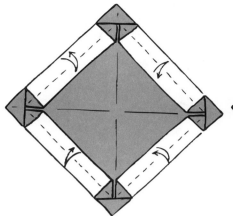

(11) Fold and unfold each of the white single layers of the long side flaps.

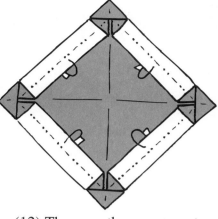

(12) Then use these creases to fold these white side flaps **inside** . . .

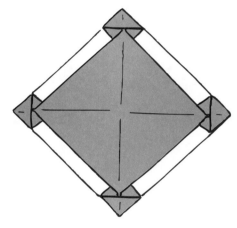

(13) . . . like this! Zoom in again on a corner.

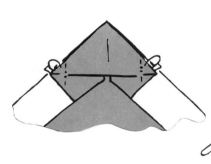

(14) Mountain-fold these small colored corners behind.

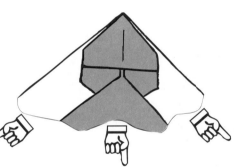

(15) See? It makes a heart! Repeat on the other corners.

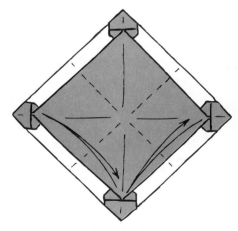

(16) Now that the hearts are done, all that's left is to make the box. Fold and unfold from side to side.

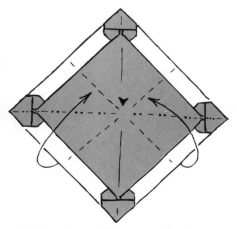

(17) Collapse, like a Preliminary Fold.

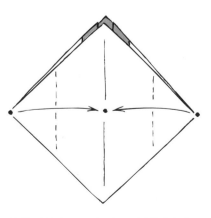

(18) (Enlarged view.) Fold the front corners to the center.

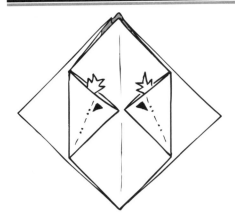
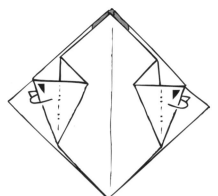
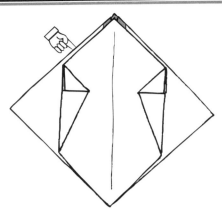

(19) Open the pockets and squash the two flaps symmetrically; watch the black triangles.

(20) Then mountain-fold the outer half of each of these flaps into the model.

(21) Cool! Repeat steps 18-20 behind.

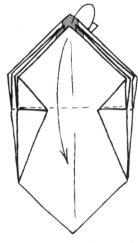
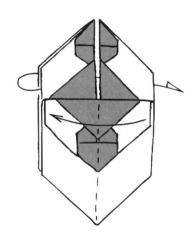
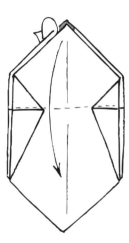

(22) Fold the top flaps down as far as possible, in front and in back.

(23) Fold a flap to the left in front, and a flap to the right in back.

(24) Repeat step 22.

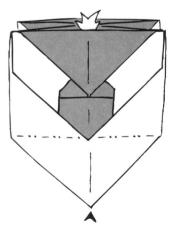
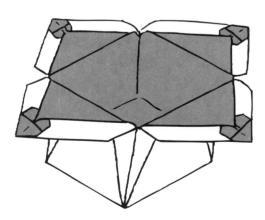

(25) Finish the model by opening up the box and flattening the bottom.

(26) The completed Four-Heart Box!

Four-Heart Dish

by Elena Afonkina

Similar in structure to the Four-Heart Box, this dish makes an elegant centerpiece, especially when folded from a large square of strong, colorful paper.

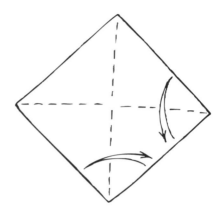

(1) White side up. Fold and unfold both diagonals.

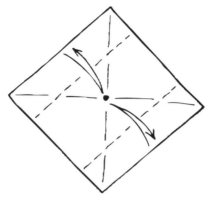

(2) Fold and unfold two sides to the center.

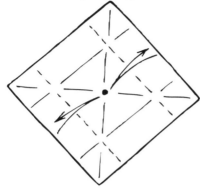

(3) Repeat this with the other two sides.

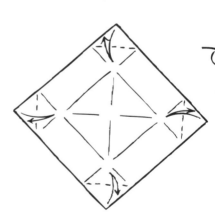

(4) Fold and unfold each corner to the nearest intersection. Turn over.

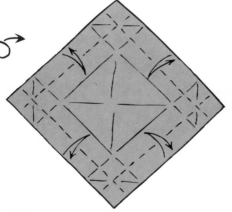

(5) Fold and unfold each side to the nearest crease line.

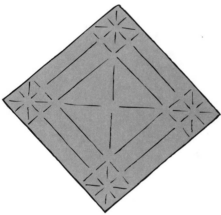

(6) Neat! Zoom in on a corner.

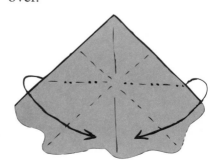

(7) Collapse the corner, and at the same time collapse the other three corners.

(8) Fold the flap up. **Repeat** with the other three corners.

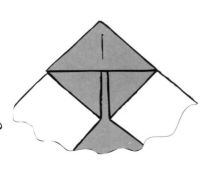

(9) OK! Zoom out.

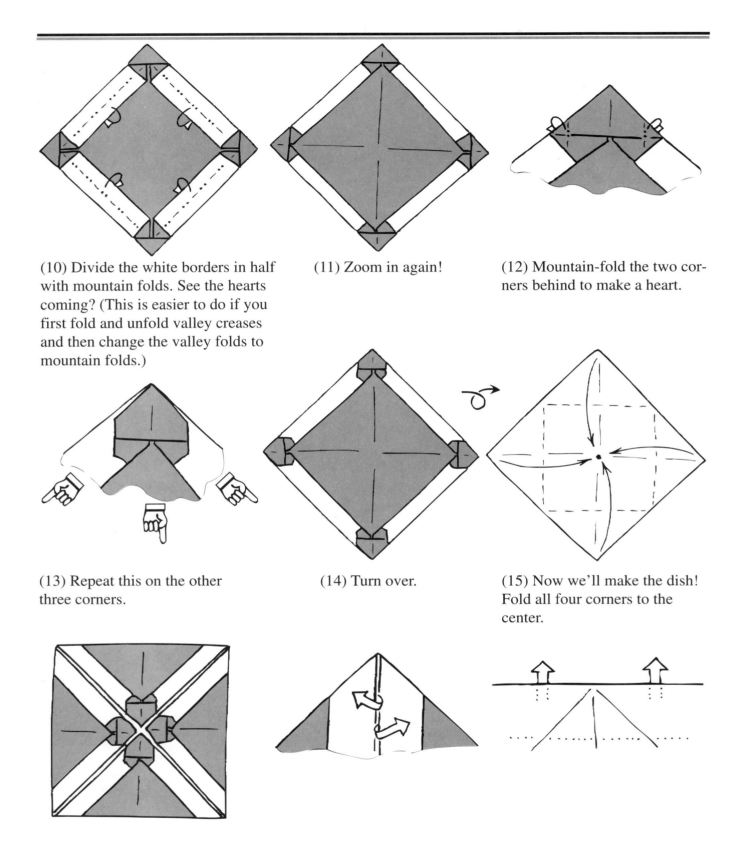

(10) Divide the white borders in half with mountain folds. See the hearts coming? (This is easier to do if you first fold and unfold valley creases and then change the valley folds to mountain folds.)

(11) Zoom in again!

(12) Mountain-fold the two corners behind to make a heart.

(13) Repeat this on the other three corners.

(14) Turn over.

(15) Now we'll make the dish! Fold all four corners to the center.

(16) Wow! Zoom in on a corner.

(17) OK. We're going to perform a tricky maneuver. Open up the corner . . .

(18) . . . and lift up the flap of paper in back . . .

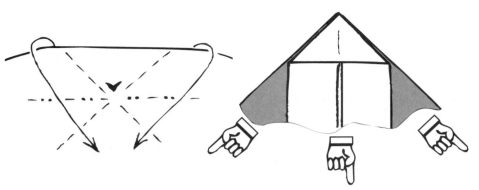

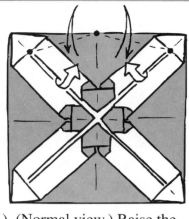

(19) . . . then push the center point in and collapse it all back down . . .

(20) . . . like this! The corner should now be kind of like a Waterbomb Base. Repeat this on the other three corners.

(21) (Normal view.) Raise the near top flap (one with a heart on it) and carefully make these two valley creases. Crease firmly and return to original position.

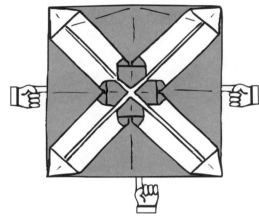

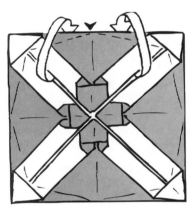

(22) Repeat step 21 on the other three sides.

(23) Now use the creases from step 21 to flip the near top flap inside-out. The creases should lock the flap into a 3-D position, and form one side of the dish . . .

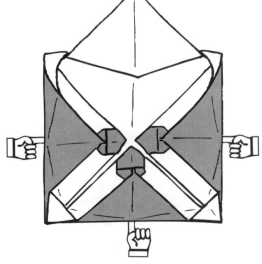

(24) . . . like this. Repeat step 23 on the other three flaps.

(25) The completed Four-Heart Dish, side and top views.

Two-Crane Box
by Elena Afonkina

Cranes are a popular subject in origami, because of their prominence in the Japanese paperfolding tradition. This box bears two decorative cranes and is folded from a 2x1 rectangle.

(1) White side up. Fold and unfold two sets of diagonals.

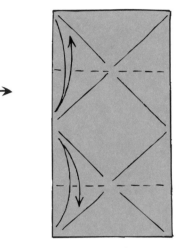

(2) Turn over and fold two horizontal creases. Turn over.

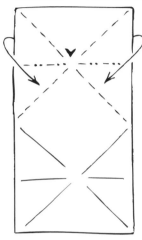

(3) Then collapse the top part into a Waterbomb Base.

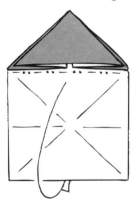

(4) Mountain-fold the rest of the paper behind.

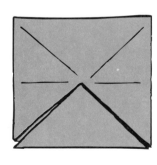

(5) Turn over.

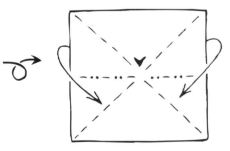

(6) Collapse this side into a Waterbomb Base.

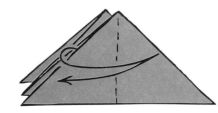

(7) Fold to the right and unfold the near left flap.

(8) Fold and unfold the same flap to the center crease.

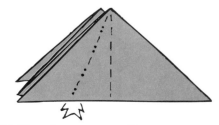

(9) Use these crease lines to open and squash the flap symmetrically.

(10) Fold and unfold the lower sides of this flap to the center line.

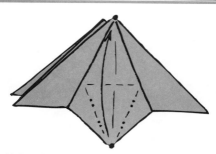

(11) Then raise the flap to the top corner, using the creases to narrow the sides . . .

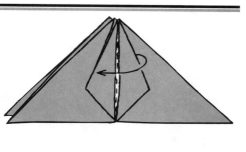

(12) . . . like so. (This is called a **petal fold**.) Fold to the left.

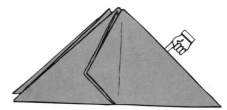

(13) Repeat steps 8-12 on the right flap.

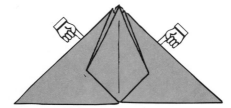

(14) Repeat steps 8-13 behind.

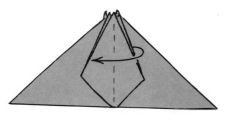

(15) Fold two small flaps to the left.

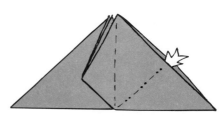

(16) Open the right flap from the top and squash it upward into a square.

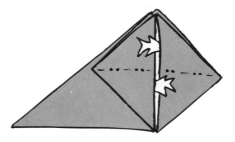

(17) Now open up the white area inside and flatten it symmetrically outward and downward . . .

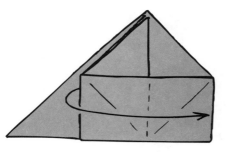

(18) . . . like this! Fold three flaps back to the right.

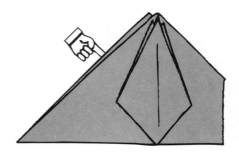

(19) Repeat steps 15-18 on the left.

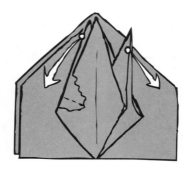

(20) Pinch the narrow right point and swivel it clockwise; flatten the model. (See step 21!) Repeat with the left point.

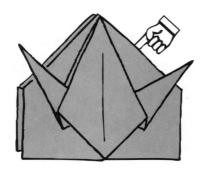

(21) Repeat step 20 behind.

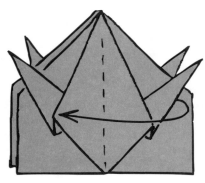

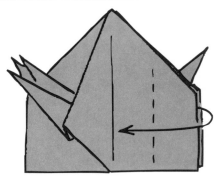

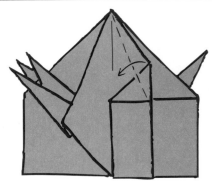

(22) Fold one of the cranes in half.

(23) Then fold one edge to the center line.

(24) Fold the top edge of the right flap to the center line, too.

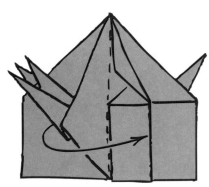

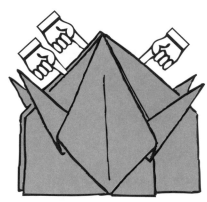

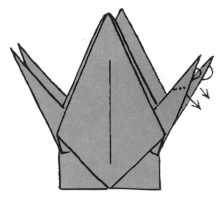

(25) Fold the half of the crane back to the right.

(26) Yeah! Now repeat steps 22-25 on the left, and behind.

(27) Reverse-fold heads for the two cranes.

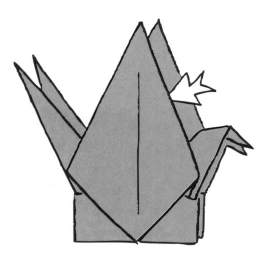

(28) Lastly, open up the middle by spreading the two cranes apart and flattening the middle into a box.

(29) The completed Two-Crane Box!

Matrioshka Doll

by Luda Lezhneva

This is the popular series of Russian dolls that fit one-inside-the-other. Luda's origami version works in the same way, but it has some difficult steps! Two squares of paper of the same size are needed to make each doll.

The Bottom Half

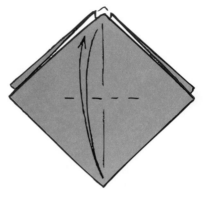

(1) Begin with a Preliminary Fold. (See page 121.) Fold one layer to the bottom, but **only pinch** a crease at the center.

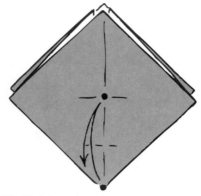

(2) Fold and unfold the bottom corner to the center point, again only pinching.

(3) Now fold and unfold the bottom corner to the previous crease line. This is a whole crease, not a pinch!

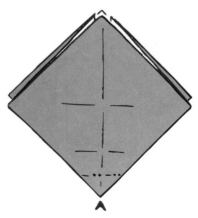

(4) All right! Using this last crease, **sink** the corner into the model. In other words, you need to invert this corner, so that it's poking inside the model. You'll need to open up the paper to make this happen.

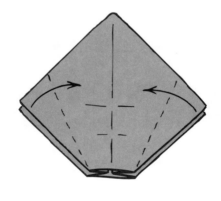

(5) This should be the result. Fold the left and right flaps in, so that the folded edges are perpendicular to the bottom edge.

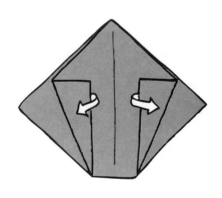

(6) Unfold step 5.

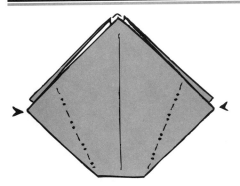

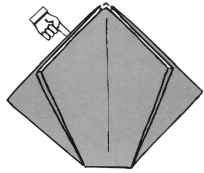

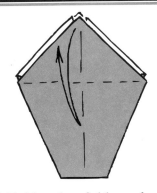

(7) Use the creases from step 5 to reverse-fold the front left and right flaps inside . . .

(8) . . . like this. Repeat steps 5-7 behind.

(9) Fold and unfold one layer.

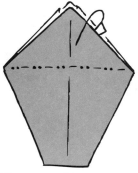

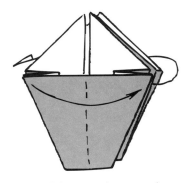

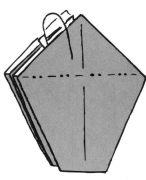

(10) Now use this crease to mountain-fold the layer directly inside. Don't cover the internal corners!

(11) Fold two edges to the right in front and two edges to the left in back.

(12) Repeat steps 9-10 with this flap.

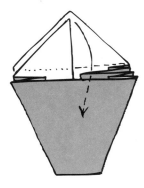

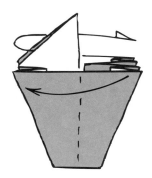

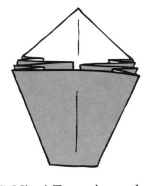

(13) Fold the back layer into the model.

(14) Fold two edges to the left in front and two to the right in back.

(15) Nice! Zoom in on the right.

(16) Mountain-fold the nearest right corner all the way into the adjoining groove.

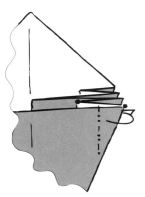

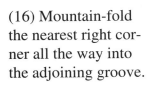

(17) Then valley-fold the next corner to meet the previous one.

(18) Do the same thing with the next two corners: Mountain-fold the near one into the groove behind.

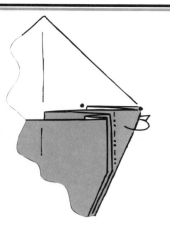

(19) Then valley-fold the last corner inside to meet the flap from step 18.

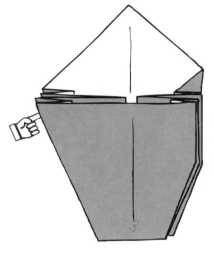

(20) Repeat steps 16-19 on the left.

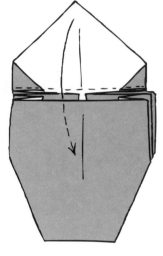

(21) Then fold the top flap inside the model, **covering all** the inside flaps.

(22) Now reverse-fold outward the inner corners at the bottom. (This will make the doll stand.)

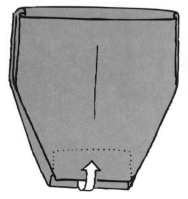

(23) Fold the bottom flap up . . .

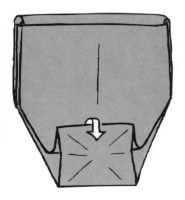

(24) . . . and fold it back down. This is only done to separate the layers so that the doll can stand.

(25) The bottom half of the Doll is finished!

The Top Half

(1) Begin with step 5 of the bottom half. Rotate 180°.

(2) Notice the X-ray view of the sunken corner. Fold up one layer at the bottom by an equal amount.

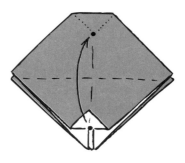

(3) Then fold the bottom layer up so that it meets this X-ray point . . .

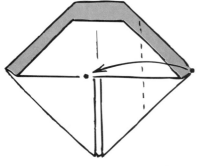

(4) . . . like this. Fold one layer to the left, along the line of the folded edge.

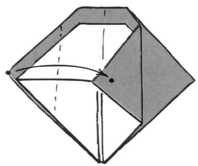

(5) Fold the left flap over as well. These "arms" should overlap.

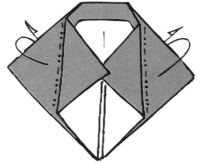

(6) Mountain-fold behind and unfold the back flaps.

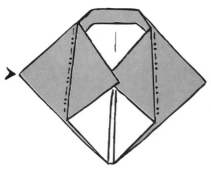

(7) Then use these creases to reverse-fold the corners inside.

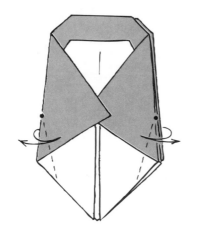

(8) Now narrow the sides a bit so that it can fit into the bottom half. Fold and unfold through **all layers**. (Test the fit with the bottom half before creasing firmly.)

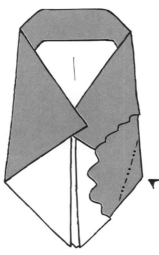

(9) (Exposed view!) Use the crease to reverse-fold inside the middle corner.

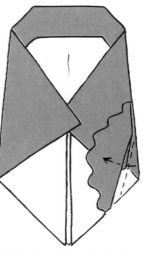

(10) Fold the back flap into the pocket you just made . . .

 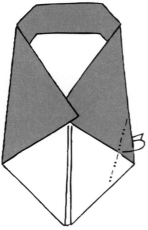  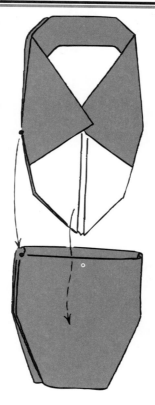

(11) . . . like this. We're finished with the exposed view.

(12) Now mountain-fold the front corner into the pocket behind it.

(13) Repeat steps 9-12 on the left, and you're done with the top half!

(14) Slide the top half into the bottom half, to complete the Matrioshka Doll.

About the Creator and the Model

Luda graduated from St. Petersburg University, Department of Russian Literature, in 1992. Luda now teaches Russian in kindergarten because she thinks that a child's first lessons in language are of the utmost importance for futher development. Usually Luda illustrates her lessons with origami models.

It's remarkable that the wooden Matrioshka toy, which is such a symbol of Russian folk culture, actually came from Japan! History tells us that in 1890 this wooden toy, depicting an old Japanese man named Fukuruma, appeared for the first time in Russia. Fukuruma's painted face was very anxious because he had to feed all of his family, which were contained inside his body! Russian craft artists turned old man Fukuruma and his family into beautiful Russian women. Isn't it fitting, that an old Japanese toy, turned into a Russian icon, can now be folded in the Japanese art of origami?

Luda Lezhneva

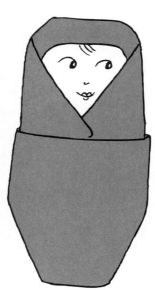

Make smaller dolls with smaller paper, say, 3/4 to 1/2 in size, and place them inside each other!

Appendix

List of Symbols

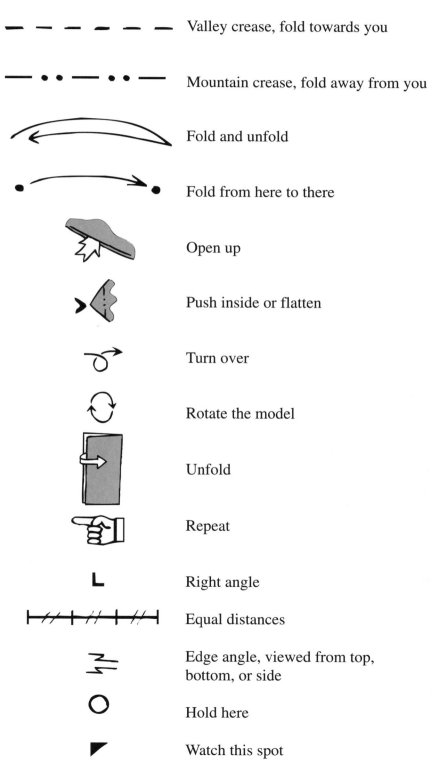

— — — — — Valley crease, fold towards you

— · · — · · — Mountain crease, fold away from you

Fold and unfold

Fold from here to there

Open up

Push inside or flatten

Turn over

Rotate the model

Unfold

Repeat

L Right angle

Equal distances

Edge angle, viewed from top, bottom, or side

O Hold here

Watch this spot

Reverse Fold

This is a very common origami maneuver that involves reversing a flap, almost turning it inside-out.

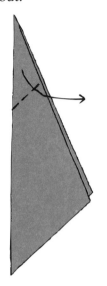 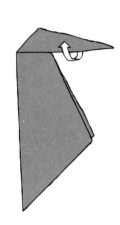  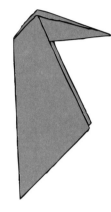

(1) To prepare for the reverse-fold, fold the point down.

(2) Crease firmly and unfold.

(3) Then use the creases you just made to reverse the point through, almost as if you were bending a soda straw . . .

(4) . . . like this!

Squash Fold

As its name suggests, this origami step involves flattening, or squashing, a flap.

(1) To squash-fold a flap, you need to raise it up and flatten it evenly. Watch the black triangle to see how this happens.

(2) This is the squash-fold in progress. The tip of the flap that is being squashed need to be brought down to the center line.

(3) The completed Squash Fold. See where the black triangle ended up?

The Preliminary Fold

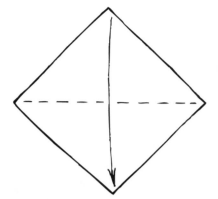

(1) White side up. Fold in half from corner to corner.

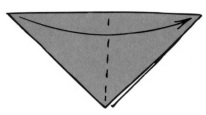

(2) Now bring the other two corners together and fold.

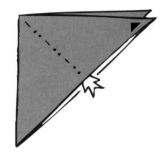

(3) Then open up one of the flaps and squash it flat into a square, bringing the near upper corner to the bottom . . .

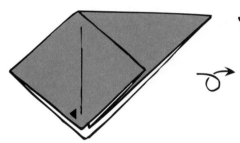

(4) . . . like this! Turn the paper over.

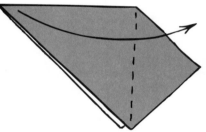

(5) Fold the left point to the right.

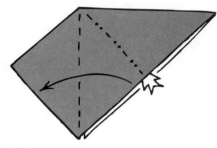

(6) Then repeat step 3 here—open up the flap and squash it flat.

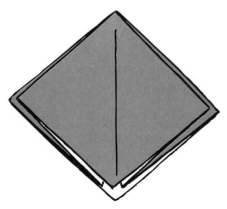

(7) The completed Preliminary Fold.

The Waterbomb Base

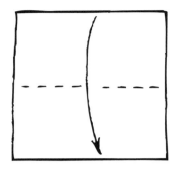

(1) White side up. Fold in half from top to bottom.

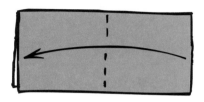

(2) Fold in half again.

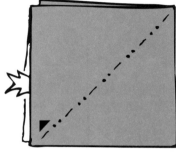

(3) (Enlarged view.) Open up one of the flaps and squash it flat into a triangle . . .

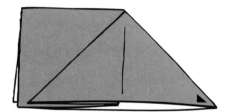

(4) . . . like this! Turn over.

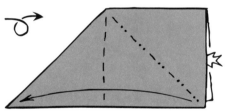

(5) Repeat step 3. That is, squash the flap into another triangle . . .

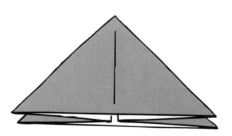

(6) . . . like this. The result is the classic Waterbomb Base!

Fun tip: Turning a Waterbomb Base inside-out will give you a Preliminary Fold. Try it!

Pinwheel Base

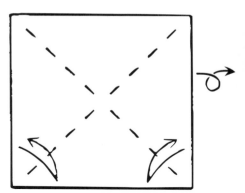

(1) White side up. Fold and unfold both diagonals. Turn over.

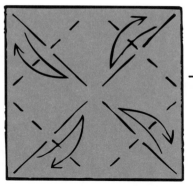

(2) Then fold the four corners to the center. Unfold and turn over again.

(3) Fold the left and right sides to the center. Unfold.

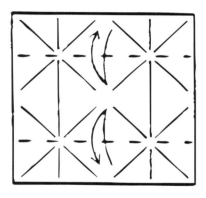

(4) Fold the top and bottom sides to the center. Unfold.

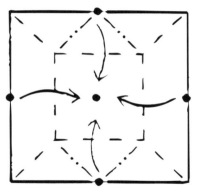

(5) Now bring the center points of the top and bottom sides to the center of the square and collapse . . .

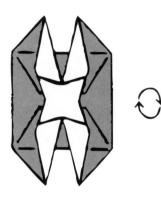

(6) . . . like this! Make sure the diagonal creases at the corners are being used. Collapse it flat and rotate 90°.

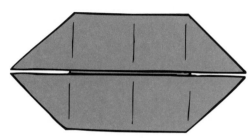

(7) The completed Pinwheel Base!

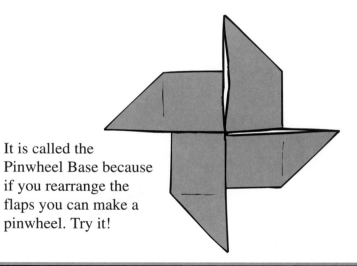

It is called the Pinwheel Base because if you rearrange the flaps you can make a pinwheel. Try it!

Acknowledgments

Big shout-outs go to Norman Prokup for providing the wonderful bear, cat & mouse, and cat cartoons (pages 33, 64, and 77), to Ramsey Piazza for letting Tom buy his computer, to Yusri Johan, Nancy and Anne Marshall, and Judith Ross McNab for trying to brainstorm a snappy title for this book, and to Cheryl Sirna for providing the thesaurus and help with diction. Ben Tyler and Gwen Kaiser need to be thanked and praised for answering Tom's frantic questions about computer assisted graphic design. The lovely Gay Merrill Gross gave us valuable consultation on Western origins of some of the models, as well as much-needed proofreading. Also, much thanks to Sam Randlett for being such an impeccable copyeditor. (23 Skidoo!)

The diagrams were tested by a number of unsuspecting victims, including Norman Prokup, Mary Beth Abel, Gay Merrill Gross, numerous guinea pigs at OrigamiUSA's 1997 Annual Convention in New York City, and Cheryl Sirna.

Sergei writes, "I am very grateful for my foreign friends who introduced me to the wonderful origami community: Dave Brill, Alfredo Giunta, Paul Jackson, Yoshihide Momotani, Paulo Mulatinho, Francis Ow, Vicente Palacios, Nilva Pillan, Nick Robinson, and Yoshio Tsuda. Also thanks to my wife Elena who helps me to dig through piles of letters that I receive every week from Russian folders."

Lastly, but not leastly, thanks to our editors Joy Chang and Tara Schimming who displayed divine patience and sympathy while one of the authors finished his Ph.D., causing him to miss many deadlines. Who says the corporate world doesn't support higher education? Hear, hear!

About the Authors

Sergei Afonkin was born September 15, 1957 in St. Petersburg, then known as Leningrad. In 1980 he graduated from St. Petersburg University's Department of Invertebrate Zoology, and in 1984 received his Ph.D. at the Institute of Cytology, Laboratory of Unicellular Organisms. Sergei did research in Russia, in Poland, and at Carmerino University in Italy. Yet during this time he felt that something was wrong in his life because, as he states, "Science was for me a very odd way to receive knowledge. Often you have to kill the living object of investigation to see what is inside (in a general sense), and I don't like to be a killer of 'little brothers.' I felt some estrangement from the people surrounding me, which was not an inspiring feeling." Then he was introduced to the art of origami. In 1991 Sergei made a sharp turn and completely changed his life. He started writing biology books for children as well as teaching in a school. Cofounding the St. Petersburg Origami Center with his wife, Elena, he began to spread the word of origami in his country. All this gave Sergei a new breath of life and the feeling that many people need his work. He writes, "After that I have felt many times that my life is arranged in heaven." Sergei and Elena have two daughters, Sandra and Dasha.

Thomas Hull was born in Rhode Island November 5, 1969 and has been folding paper since he was eight years old, when his mysterious Uncle Paul gave Tom his first origami book. In addition to origami Tom became fascinated with mathematics, graduating from Hampshire College in 1991 with a concentration in complex dynamics and fractal geometry. Soon after entering graduate school at the University of Rhode Island, he began to see his two passions converge. After absorbing the work on the mathematics of origami by origami mathematicians Toshikazu Kawasaki, Jacques Justin, Jun Maekawa and others, Tom began his own research on the subject; he has published several technical papers, and articles about his origami-math work have appeared in *Yankee Magazine* and in *Science News*. In 1994 he lectured in Japan at the 2nd International Meeting of Origami Science and Scientific Origami, and in the same year Tom's first origami book was published: *Origami, Plain and Simple*—a collection of models by Robert Neale. Tom has since lectured all over the world on the joys of origami-math. While writing *Russian Origami* Tom completed his Ph.D. in mathematics at

Nancy Marshall

the University of Rhode Island, writing his dissertation about list colorings (a subject in graph theory, with no real relation to origami, unfortunately). He is currently an assistant professor of mathematics at Merrimack College, and plans to write his next book on the mathematics of origami.

Author Index